JOHN E.
PARSONS

JOHN E. PARSONS

An Eminent New Yorker
in the Gilded Age

Paul DeForest Hicks

PROSPECTA PRESS

WESTPORT AND NEW YORK
2016

Published by Prospecta Press, an imprint of Easton Studio Press
P.O. Box 3131
Westport, CT 06880
(203) 571-0781
www.prospectapress.com
Designed by Barbara Aronica-Buck

First Edition
Manufactured in the United States of America
Hardcover ISBN: 978-1-63226-073-4
eBook ISBN: 978-1-63226-074-1

To Barbara, my muse and resident editor

Acknowledgments

I particularly appreciate the many helpful insights David Parsons has shared with me about his great-grandfather's personal and family life in New York City, Rye and Lenox. Cornelia ("Nini") Gilder has played an equally valuable role in helping me discover aspects of Lenox and the Berkshires that were so important to Parsons and his family, and Suky Werman has added to my appreciation of Parsons's love of that area.

I am grateful to numerous individuals, who helped me uncover details about significant aspects of Parsons's multi-faceted career, especially Jeffrey Januzzo and Professor Daniel Sharfstein for their suggestions about law practice and legal history; Harry Havemeyer for his personal account of his grandfather, Henry O. Havemeyer (the driving force behind the Sugar Trust); Professor Peter Buckley and Carol Saloman for the history of Cooper Union; Dr. William Schneider and Kathleen Brennan for the early years of Memorial Sloan Kettering Cancer Center as well as Dr. Lawrence Koblenz for his research on the history of cancer treatment.

Through access to the Parsons's papers in the archives of the Rye Historical Society, Sheri Jordan (Executive Director) and her staff have provided me with the primary source materials that are so important for any historian, amateur or professional. Suzanne Clary, president of

viii ACKNOWLEDGMENTS

the Jay Heritage Center in Rye, contributed to my understanding of life in Westchester County during the Gilded Age, when the Jay and Parsons families were next-door neighbors.

My thanks go also to my fellow author, Robert Pennoyer, for introducing me to David Wilk, who has guided me through the editing and publishing process with professional skill and unfailing good cheer.

Contents

Introduction

The Gilded Age (roughly 1870 to 1910) was a period of rapid economic growth in the U.S. that resulted in a great divide between the "haves" and "have-nots." Today's super-rich "one percent" and the growing income inequality in the country are often cited as evidence that we are in the midst of a second Gilded Age. Over-compensated CEOs, hedge-fund managers and Wall Street traders are seen as latter-day versions of the robber barons who manipulated the nation's economy through speculation and corporate consolidations (widely known as "trusts").

There were many successful speculators and heads of large trusts at the turn of the twentieth century, but books about that era have focused mainly on a small number of famous tycoons and the business sectors they dominated. Among the most notable were Andrew Carnegie (steel), Jay Gould (railroads), J. P. Morgan (finance) and John D. Rockefeller (oil). They were, however, only four of the 750 millionaires in New York City (3,500 nationwide) who were listed in the 1902 edition of Hearst's *World Almanac*.

Adjusted for inflation, $1 million in 1902 was roughly equivalent to $25 million today, so those included on the *World Almanac* list were really multi-millionaires. Most of them were industrialists, merchants, financiers, real estate investors or heirs of large estates.

However, the rising tide of income, especially in New York, had elevated a small number of leading attorneys to millionaire status. Among them was John E. Parsons, one of the most eminent lawyers of the Gilded Age.

Parsons was still actively practicing law at age seventy-nine in 1908 when the *New York Times* described him as "New Yorker born and bred, legal advisor to big corporations and estates, and as a lawyer, believed to have the finest practice in the country." He was reputed to have received one of the largest fees ever earned by a lawyer when he drew up the charter of the Sugar Trust in 1887. Winning the "Sugar Trust" case, a landmark antitrust action decided by the U.S. Supreme Court in 1895, added significantly to his reputation as well as his income.

Many clients of Parsons were on the 1902 list of millionaires, including the Astors, Coopers, Dodges, Havemeyers, Hewitts and Lorillards. They were all pillars of New York society, led by Mrs. William Astor, who was widely recognized as the doyenne of the social elite (the famous "400"). Those who could trace their descent from the original Dutch settlers (including Parsons) were generally referred to as "Old Knickerbockers," whose fashions and foibles were memorably depicted in Edith Wharton's *The Age of Innocence*.

None of his clients benefitted more from his legal skills than Henry O. (Harry) Havemeyer, who was the driving force behind the Sugar Trust. As its general counsel for more than twenty-five years, Parsons dealt with some of the most important and contentious political and economic issues of the period. Whether he was trying cases, arguing appeals or dealing with legislative committees about trusts, tariffs, rebates, campaign finance and other Sugar Trust matters, Parsons remained a favorite subject of reporters and columnists.

Over his long career, the legal profession underwent enormous changes, yet Parsons adapted and continued his remarkable record of success well into his seventies. The business revolution not only gave birth to the modern corporation, it also spawned the modern corporate attorney. Along with other elite lawyers like Joseph H. Choate, William Nelson Cromwell, Elihu Root, John W. Sterling and Francis Lynde Stetson, Parsons was in the front rank of attorneys who, as counselors, managed to steer their clients clear of litigation whenever possible.

In a memorial tribute to Parsons, Choate wrote: "Mr. Parsons was the ablest and most accomplished all-round lawyer I have ever encountered . . . There is no branch of the law or equity in which he was not fully equipped, but outside of court too he was a great lawyer, and I believe one of the wisest, most sagacious, and safest legal advisers that we ever had."

He also played a major role in strengthening New York's legal profession, which suffered after the Civil War both from relaxation of rules for bar admission and from a lack of organization and leadership. Corrupt actions by judicial allies of the notorious Boss Tweed finally convinced leading lawyers to form the Bar Association of the City of New York in 1871. Parsons, one of the youngest members of the original executive committee, took on an extensive investigation of three Tweed judges, which led to the impeachment of two and resignation of the third.

Although he avoided partisan politics and never sought public office, Parsons was a long-time leader of the nonpartisan movement to eliminate corruption and achieve political reform in New York City. Describing himself to a *New York Times* reporter in 1910 as an "old-time Democrat," he believed in "recognition of the rights of the

State as against attempted usurpation by the Federal Government."

In addition to serving for more than five decades on the board of Cooper Union, Parsons headed the boards of two pioneering hospitals. One was the New York Woman's Hospital, founded in 1857 as the first hospital in America dedicated exclusively to treating female patients. He also led the board of what is now Memorial Sloan Kettering Cancer Center from its founding in 1882 and guided it through its turbulent early years up to his death.

Despite his demanding legal, civic and charitable commitments, Parsons took great pleasure in his private life, spending as much time as possible with his devoted wife Mary and their children in New York City as well as at their country homes. His boyhood home on a large estate in Rye, New York, allowed him to satisfy his taste for rural life on weekends and short vacations. Also, as long-time summer residents of Lenox in the Berkshires, the Parsons were among the early "cottagers," who came there in search of a healthy place for their children, far removed from urban problems.

The death of his merchant father in a shipwreck when Parsons was not yet ten instilled in him the discipline and self-reliance for which he was widely admired. At age eighty, Parsons's strength of character enabled him to bear the stress of being tried, along with other directors of the Sugar Trust, for alleged criminal violations of the antitrust law.

The conclusion of Joseph Choate's memorial tribute in the City Bar Yearbook expressed a widely held view of John E. Parsons: "It would be hard to find in the whole ranks of our profession a more upright and honorable example of true service than the whole history of his life affords, and his name deserves to be cherished forever in this Association, as one of the most zealous founders and most valuable members and servants."

JOHN E.
PARSONS

Chapter One
Shipwreck

Keeping to its schedule, the packet ship *Pennsylvania* sailed down the Mersey River from Liverpool on Christmas Day of 1838, bound for New York. Advertised as a "fast vessel with commodious and elegantly outfitted cabins," the ship was carrying five passengers and a crew of thirty-five in addition to royal mail and a cargo of fine goods. Among its passengers was a merchant, Edward Lamb Parsons, who had written to his wife Matilda shortly before his departure:

> My Loving Wife,
>
> As the *Royal William* sails the day after tomorrow, I write thee perhaps for the last time till I see thee for I have taken my passage on the ship *Pennsylvania* which is to sail the 25th —a large and most beautiful ship, well-commanded and which will, I trust, have its usual good fortune in getting home . . . I pray God who rules the elements to bring me safe again to those shores, thy arms and embraces from the little ones . . .
>
> Yr Devoted Husband

Wreck of the packet ship *Pennsylvania* (courtesy of David Parsons)

Calm weather required the *Pennsylvania* to remain for more than a week at the mouth of the Mersey River, waiting for a favorable wind. A contemporary account described what happened soon after the wind finally shifted and the ship sailed into the Irish Sea on that fateful voyage:

On the 12th day of Christmas (January 6, 1839), the day was fine; a fair wind blew for outward-bound ships. Many of them left the Mersey under sail, among them the *St. Andrew*, *the Lockwood* and the *Pennsylvania*, first-class packet ships, loaded with valuable cargoes and emigrants, together with a few saloon passengers for New York. On the morning of the 7th, the barometer fell to a very low point. The vessels had almost reached Holyhead [an island off the coast of Wales] when suddenly the wind changed to the north-west and blew a hurricane.

According to another report:

As the storm continued unabated for two days, the ship turned back toward Liverpool, plotting a course for the Mersey lightship. Unknown to the *Pennsylvania*, however, the floating light had parted from its mooring the previous day. Before an anchor could be dropped the vessel swung around, drifted, and struck the Hoyle Bank. The force of the gale rammed her into the bank eight or nine times, and she started to take on water rapidly . . . two other packet ships, the *St. Andrew* and the *Lockwood* also struck the Bank, not more than half a mile apart.

In an attempt to reach the shore, the *Pennsylvania's* jolly boat was launched into the gale . . . Only one of its occupants survived. Meanwhile back on the wreck of the *Pennsylvania*, the long boat, the only other prospect of escape, was lost in heavy waves, which also swept the Captain overboard . . . The remaining crew climbed desperately into the rigging where they were to cling for dear life for nineteen hours. It was not until ten am the next day that the steam tug *Victoria* took them off, except that is, three of the crew who had literally been starved to death of cold and hunger in the rigging during the night. Twenty-one were saved from the wreck, nineteen drowned.

A Liverpool newspaper, describing the scene of devastation after the wreck of all three packets, reported that the beach was covered with wreckage and dead bodies. It identified one of the victims as "Mr. Edward Lamb Parsons, a merchant of New York, tall, slender make and fashionably dressed," adding that he had "a considerable amount of property on him." After the inquest, his body was taken by some of his business friends and buried in his native city of Manchester.

Born in 1805, Edward Parsons left England in his late teens to join the New York sales office of his family's cotton thread manufacturing firm. After his father's death in 1823, he became the principal representative of the family's interests in America and prospered from the growing imports of cotton thread. The business required him to make a number of visits to England and Scotland to satisfy the demand for thread in America, especially from makers of women's fashions.

In 1827, at the age of twenty-two, he married Matilda Clark, a daughter of Ebenezer and Anna Marselis Clark, at her family's church in Rye, New York. Like most business and professional New Yorkers of the period, Edward and his young family first lived in lower Manhattan near his firm's office. He was naturalized as an American citizen in 1830, and by 1831, he had accumulated enough capital to buy a summer home with nearly forty acres of farmland in Rye, New York, paying $5,500. The property had been advertised for sale in the *New York Evening Post* a few years earlier as a:

> Farm or Country Seat adjoining the estate of Peter Jay, Esq., situated on Rye Neck, West Chester County, twenty-four miles from the city of New York, it contains about thirty seven acres, six or seven of which are woodland, several are salt meadow and sedge, and the residue excellent meadow and plough land. The buildings, consisting of a mansion, farm and carriage house, barn, granary, crib, milk house, etc. are substantially built and nearly new; the fences are of stone, and for strength and appearance are probably not surpassed, and perhaps not equaled by those on any other farm of equal size in this state . . .
>
> The situation of this farm and its vicinity are peculiarly healthy, and the dwelling house occupying the highest ground on Rye Neck, commands a view of forty or fifty miles of Long Island Sound. The farm is bounded in front by the mail road leading from New York to Boston, and extends to the salt water. Shell and scale fish of all or most of the varieties usually taken in the Sound, abound in the neighborhood, and several

birds may be caught in great plenty in the waters immediately adjoining the farm. Marine wild fowl are also abundant in their season, and other feathered game sufficient to attract the attention of those who are partial to the amusement of fowling. This farm is calculated to suit those who would wish to enjoy the pleasures of a country life without the cares incident to a large farm . . .

As his wealth grew, Edward decided to enlarge the home on their country estate, which was completed shortly before he left for England in October of 1838. Designed in the Greek revival style with fluted Ionic columns on its main façade, the three-story residence became an attractive landmark for those traveling on the Post Road between New York and Boston. Because it incorporated part of the farm house that had been on the property since colonial times, Edward named the residence "Lounsberry" (sometimes spelled "Lounsbury") after the family who were early owners of the property.

It is likely that Edward and Matilda chose an architectural design for their new home that would be compatible with the handsome new home, built the prior year by the parents of Matilda about a mile to the north.

It also harmonized with the next-door mansion of Peter Clarkson Jay, called "Alansten," which was also designed in the Greek revival style and replaced a much simpler house that had been the childhood home of Peter's father, Chief Justice John Jay. The Parsons and Jay properties are now part of a National Historic Landmark District.

According to Suzanne Clary, head of the Jay Heritage Center: "Long before he inherited the property outright, John Jay treated it like his own, maintaining gardens, planting trees, and establishing, in 1807, a tranquil cemetery lined with cypresses for himself, his siblings, and descendants. Together with his son Peter Augustus Jay, he oversaw the installation of gardens and elm tree plantings in Rye.

"He guided his son's introduction of stone ha-ha walls in 1822 as a means to frame not only the landscape, but specifically the wide open meadow that stretched to the water. The ha-ha walls served many functional as well as aesthetic purposes including an uninterrupted view of the water from the mansion [and] a formalized Palladian vista of the estate from the Sound . . ."

Edward could feel comfortable leaving his family at Lounsberry, knowing they were well settled in their new home and that they would be looked after by family and friends. During his absence, Matilda remained in Rye with their two youngest children (Mary was not yet two and Arthur was still an infant). The three older ones (Anna, John and William, ages ten, nine and seven) went to stay in Connecticut with Matilda's sister and her husband, who took charge of their schooling.

News of the terrible shipwrecks and loss of life in the hurricane of January 6 and 7, 1839, did not reach New York until February 12, when the packet ship *Cambridge* arrived from Liverpool. The February 16 issue of *Niles' Weekly Register*, a widely read national news magazine, carried a detailed and gruesome account of the disaster. Although it reported that "twenty-six persons had been rescued from the *Pennsylvania*," none of the names were listed and the number of survivors differed from other reports.

When the *Royal William* reached New York in mid-January with Edward's letter, Matilda would have learned of his plans to sail for New York on Christmas Day aboard the *Pennsylvania*. However, it is not known how long she had to wait until she learned of his fate. Since the *Cambridge* left Liverpool on January 10, it is possible that Edward's business friends or family in England had time to send her a letter by that packet, telling her of his death and burial.

Even though news of Edward's death was devastating for Matilda, she had received a premonition in January while a friend was visiting her at Lounsberry. As confirmed by that friend to her son John many years later, Matilda was very much disturbed one evening by the noise of a bird in a tree at the front of the house, so the friend went outside to investigate, taking a fowling piece with him. He shortly returned with a white dove he had shot, which must have escaped from the family's dovecote. When he told her that she would not be troubled by the noise any more, she said she feared it was an ill omen.

The death of Edward in the prime of his life thrust adult responsibilities on his eldest son, John, at an early age and had a profound effect throughout his life. It was not until 1901, more than sixty years after the shipwreck, that John was able to remove his father's remains from the cemetery in Manchester for reburial in a family vault at Rye. That final reuniting of the family helped him bring closure to a painful and enduring experience.

Chapter Two
Early Years

The years John Parsons spent as a boy at his family's Lounsberry estate in Rye instilled in him a lasting love for country life and rural communities. It also helped to keep alive memories of his father, who, as he once wrote, had an Englishman's love of the countryside. Although Edward Parsons became a naturalized American citizen, he wanted to maintain ties with England for the benefit of himself and his family.

Once the construction of Lounsberry was completed, Edward planned to acquire an additional home in England where he could stay during business trips and house his family when they joined him. During his trip there in the fall of 1838, he wrote to Matilda, "As to our future residence here, London or its area will suit us much the best . . . the country is fine, and the cottages and dwellings large . . . I think we can manage to contain all the comfort and independence of our own house without its trouble or the necessity of always stopping at houses."

He took time during his business travels to explore the possibility of having John attend one of the English boarding (called "public") schools. The caliber of education then available at the better public

Matilda Clark Parsons (courtesy of Rye Historical Society)

schools like Eton, Harrow and Rugby, would have been superior to most of the secondary schools in the New York area. Moreover, an English public school education could provide useful connections for John as he prepared for a career in the family's Anglo-American trading firm.

If Edward had lived, he might have sent John to Rugby School, located not far from his family's ancestral home town of Cubbington in the county of Warwickshire (not far from Stratford-upon-Avon). Rugby's headmaster, Dr. Thomas Arnold, had recently introduced educational reforms that were gaining wide recognition for him and the school. Although Arnold put a high value on learning, he believed that the greater goal in a boy's education was the formation of his character.

Edward's death ruled out English schooling for John, which might have led him down a far different path in life than the one he took. In many respects, however, the religious, moral and intellectual guidance he received in his youth from his grandfather, Ebenezer Clark, and other family members was based on the same Victorian principles as those of Dr. Arnold.

Ebenezer Clark was born in 1769 and raised in Wallingford, Connecticut, where his colonial forbears had settled in the late 1600s. He moved to New York City as a young man and started in business as a coach maker, the first step in a long and successful career as a merchant. In 1796, he married Annetje (Anna) Marselis, a member of an old New York family who traced their lineage back to Dutch settlers who arrived in New Netherland in the 1660s.

The Marselis family's "Knickerbocker" (Dutch colonial) ancestry would prove to be especially valuable later in life for John Parsons as he made his mark in the social and professional worlds of the Gilded Age in the late-nineteenth century. It was then that one of his prominent law clients, Mrs. William Astor (born Caroline Schermerhorn), headed the list of the "first four hundred" in New York Society, which included many other family names of Dutch origin, including Stuyvesant, Roosevelt, de Peyster, and Van Rensselaer.

Like other prosperous New Yorkers in the early 1800s, the Clark family resided in lower Manhattan, moving from Broad Street eventually to the corner of Broadway and Houston. William E. Dodge, a close friend of John Parsons who lived in that area as a young man recalled later in his life that "the Battery was the great point of attraction as a cool and delightful promenade, and in the warm season was crowded every afternoon and evening; the grass was kept clean and green and the walks in perfect order . . . In the summer and early fall a band of music in the evening enlivened the scene, and the grounds were crowded with the elite of the city . . ."

Although the harbor views and breezes at Bowling Green and walks along the tree-lined paths in City Hall Park made urban life more bearable, residents still had to put up with the noise, smells and dirt of urban life. The better neighborhoods expanded steadily northwards. According to Dodge, however, "There were no police in those days, but there were a few watchmen, who came on soon after dark and patrolled the streets till near daylight. Their rounds were so arranged that they made one each hour, and as the clocks struck they pounded with their clubs three times on the curb, calling out, for example, 'Twelve o'clock, and all is well,' in a very peculiar voice."

The nearby neighborhood known as Five Points, named for the intersection of five streets, was developing from what was once a desirable residential area into a slum that would later became a notorious center of crime and gang violence. Then in 1819, an epidemic of yellow fever that claimed dozens of lives convinced the Clarks to seek a healthier life for their invalid son and four daughters outside the city.

In 1821, they moved to the Town of Rye in rural Westchester County, close enough to the city so Ebenezer could still look after his business interests from time to time. Susan Fenimore Cooper, daughter of the famous novelist, told in her memoir of growing up in the nearby towns of Mamaroneck and Scarsdale in the early 1820s. She wrote that when her father needed to meet with a printer or publisher in New York, he traveled the twenty-five miles to the city, "sometimes by the Mamaroneck stage, sometimes in his gig, occasionally on horseback."

Named for a town in the south of England, Rye was settled in 1660 by colonists who had moved there from the nearby settlement at Greenwich, Connecticut. According to the historic records, they purchased an area lying along the shore of Long Island Sound from the local Siwanoy band of Lenape Indians for "eight cotes, seven shirts, and fifteen fathoms of wampum." The following year another tract of land was acquired from the Siwanoys, which included the Lounsberry acres that were subsequently purchased by Edward Parsons.

During the Revolutionary War, the residents of Rye lived in what was known as the "Neutral Ground," enduring many raids, skirmishes and other hardships caused alternately by British troops, Tory sympathizers, patriots and outlaws. The troubled times were captured by James Fenimore Cooper in his popular novel, *The Spy: a Tale of the Neutral Ground.*

Set in Westchester County, the story is loosely based on the exploits of actual American intelligent agents who spied on Tory loyalists, including members of the Lounsberry family. Cooper is said to have conceived the idea for the story from his friend, John Jay, who was responsible for the American counterintelligence activities in the early stages of the war.

Memories of the war were still fresh in the minds of older Rye residents when John Parsons was a boy, giving him vivid accounts of the sacrifices the older generations had made to win independence. Later in life, he acknowledged that the example of John Jay, who was buried in the family cemetery on the adjoining Jay property, had been a major influence on his choice of a legal career.

In the census of 1800, the population of Rye numbered just under 1,000 inhabitants, but two decades later the town's population had increased to 1,342, including 177 who worked in agriculture, 80 in manufacturing and 35 in commerce. The economy of the area had recovered slowly from the disruption of the War of 1812, but was beginning to show signs of prosperity by the time Matilda Clark married Edward Parsons in 1827, followed by the birth of their son John in 1829.

A sketch of Rye, as it existed around 1840 (when John was not yet in his teens), was included in *Chronicle of a Border Town—History of Rye, Westchester County, New York, 1660–1870*, written by Rev. Charles W. Baird in 1871:

> Thirty years ago, this was still a secluded village, separated by a journey of several hours from the stir and thrift of the city. The houses number about thirty-five or forty. The Boston mail passes through daily. A steamboat touches every

week-day at Rye Port, to and from New York . . . Rye is much resorted to in summer by citizens of New York. There is no regular hotel, or place of entertainment . . . The post-office is kept in the "Square House," one of the oldest houses in the place . . . It stands on the post-road in the village . . . near the 26 mile stone . . .

In 1836, Ebenezer Clark and his family moved from a comfortable dwelling into a spacious new home in the small Village of Rye that was part of the larger Town of Rye. Running through their estate was Blind Brook, a tidal stream that emptied into a harbor on Long Island Sound where it was bordered by the properties owned by the Jay and Parsons families. By timing the tidal flows correctly, it would have been an easy journey for the Parsons children to travel by canoe or skiff between the homes of their parents and grandparents, instead of going on horseback or by carriage.

A staunch Presbyterian, Ebenezer Clark discovered upon his arrival in Rye that the local congregation had been on the wane ever since the Revolution. A history of the Rye Presbyterian Church quotes from a manuscript in the church files describing the conditions in Rye about the time of Clark's arrival: "At that period . . . the people were in no sense religious . . . attendance at public worship was not the order of things; and the Sabbath day seemed to have scarcely any other use than listless idleness or application to vain pursuits . . ."

However, with the moral leadership and financial support of Clark, the Presbyterians began to be revitalized, hiring Williams Howe Whittemore as their new minister in 1829. The church became the center of John's closely-knit family, especially when the Rev. Whittemore married his mother's sister, Maria.

One of the reasons for the growth in membership was the popularity of its Sunday school, in which John Parsons was enrolled from an early age. When he was working as a young lawyer in New York City in the 1850s, he drew on his own experience to start a mission Sunday school for children living on the Lower East Side, acting as its supervisor for more than twenty years.

When a new Rye Presbyterian church was built in 1841, Ebenezer Clark provided 5,000 of the 6,000 dollars required for its construction. It is likely that he also had a strong say in the selection of its architectural style, a classical Greek temple with four Doric columns, since it harmonized with his home, located directly across the street.

After his death in 1847, one of his admirers wrote of Ebenezer Clark: "He was not swayed from his convictions of truth and duty, was outspoken in his sentiments, had no patience with idleness and vice, much less with dishonesty; and yet was he kind toward the erring and ever forward to provide for the poor. There was an honest candor about him, verging on bluntness, at times amusing as it was timely . . ."

For John Parsons, his grandfather's character, especially his firm commitment to religious, philanthropic and civic principles, had a strong and lasting influence. Clark also provided financial security for Matilda and her children when the surviving partners of Edward Parsons lost more than one-half of his estate's investment in the firm. To reduce costs, Matilda leased Lounsberry for several years and moved her primary residence to New York, but she and her children frequently stayed with her parents in Rye.

She was also able, with her father's help, to have John educated at a school in Rye run by her brother-in-law, Samuel Underhill Berrian. A Latin and Greek scholar as well as a published authority on grammar, Berrian was married to Edward Parsons's sister, Eliza Parsons. After teaching classes for several years at an historic building in the Village of Rye, known as the "Square House," Berrian opened a school at his home for boarding and day students in 1834. Called the Christomathic Institute, he ran it successfully for many years and attracted students from a wide area.

Berrian took a special interest in the intellectual development of John. Writing to Matilda in 1842, he described John as "a spontaneous and voluntary student, which is saying a great deal for any boy in this age of lax exertion . . . he has added Greek to his Latin and is making good improvement in both." A year later, he wrote Matilda that, "I have never in my twenty years as a public school instructor, had a pupil better grounded in Latin and Greek . . . than he has at his present age . . . His standing in Mathematics is almost as good . . ."

The loving support he received from his extended family helped John to overcome the loss of his father and develop the maturity that, combined with his intellectual talent, enabled him to enter college just short of his fifteenth birthday. He was leaving the simple and secure life of rural Rye, for the complexities and challenges of undergraduate life in New York City, which Washington Irving had nicknamed "Gotham," after a city in England whose residents had a reputation for madness and trickery.

Chapter Three
A Gotham Education

Whuen John Parsons finished secondary school in 1844 he was only fourteen, but his uncle and schoolmaster, Samuel Berrian, was sure that he had the academic ability and maturity to do well in college. A year earlier, Berrian had written Matilda Parsons that her son was already better prepared for college than one of his older students who had just gained advanced standing at Yale.

In addition to Yale, a likely choice for Parsons might have been Princeton (then known as the College of New Jersey), whose strong ties to the Presbyterian Church would have pleased his grandfather. However, it was a long trip to both New Haven and Princeton in the days before railroad connections, and Matilda must have preferred to have him educated somewhere nearer to her and his siblings in New York City.

Columbia would also have been a likely choice, because of its history (its name had been changed from King's College after the Revolution) and its convenient location, which was then near the present site of City Hall. If he needed a recommendation for Columbia, Parsons could have received one from their Rye neighbor, Dr. John

UNIVERSITY OF THE CITY OF NEW YORK.

View of the University of the City of New York, circa 1850 (courtesy of New York Public Library)

Clarkson Jay, who had inherited the family estate when his father, Peter Augustus Jay, died in 1843. Like his grandfather, John Jay, and his father, Dr. Jay was an alumnus of Columbia College as well as of its medical school, the College of Physicians and Surgeons.

The prospect of Parsons enrolling at Columbia would not have appealed to a staunch Calvinist like Ebenezer Clark in view of its heavy emphasis on teaching classics to students destined for careers in the Episcopal clergy. Even worse was the possibility that Parsons might be influenced to abandon the Presbyterian Church and become an Episcopalian, as was the case with the noted diarist, George Templeton Strong, who attended Columbia during the 1830s.

Ultimately, it was decided that Parsons should attend the University of the City of New York (renamed New York University in 1896), which offered an innovative alternative to the more traditional colleges. When NYU was chartered in 1831, the founders planned to build a university that would capitalize on the intellectual and cultural resources of New York City while admitting students on merit and not on the basis of family background or sectarian beliefs. It remained, nonetheless, predominantly a Christian and Protestant institution for many years.

A prospectus published for the new university in 1832 stated that the curriculum was developed for students who "are designed for the more practical pursuits of life, and who would desire to become masters of those branches of knowledge most immediately connected with their respective professions or employments." Despite the different approaches to curriculum and admissions taken by NYU, the new university was seen as a serious threat by the administration and trustees of Columbia. Attempts to persuade the state legislature to deny a charter to NYU were unsuccessful, and it received broad support from business, financial and professional leaders in New York City.

Nonetheless, NYU got off to a rocky start when Albert Gallatin, the first president of the university council (board of trustees), resigned after serving only one year. He was frustrated that the Chancellor, Reverend James Matthews, was not moving quickly enough to combine the classical curriculum with more modern subjects. Also, the fiscally conservative Gallatin opposed using a large part of NYU's meager endowment to purchase land on the east side of Washington Square as the site for the university's main building.

Washington Square had only recently been converted from a potter's field to a military parade ground and public park when construction of the large neo-Gothic University Building was begun. In spite of cost overruns, battles with city officials and a riot by stone cutters, the building was completed in 1835. Influenced by the architectural style of Oxford and Cambridge, it housed all of NYU's academic and administrative facilities, including a library that provided space for the New York Historical Society's collection for a number of years.

In order to obtain much-needed revenue, NYU rented unused space in the upper part of the University Building to some remarkable academic and artistic tenants who taught courses and added luster to the university's faculty. Most notable was the inventor and painter, Samuel F. B. Morse, whose first successful demonstration of the telegraph occurred there in 1838. As one historian describes the time and place: "Over the years, these floors became a combination of apartment house, scientific laboratory, clubhouse of the Hudson River School and haven for one of the city's earliest bohemian communities."

Around Washington Square a growing number of stylish row

houses were built and occupied in the 1830s by some of New York's most substantial families. Henry James, who was born at 21 Washington Place in 1843, described one such home in his novel, *Washington Square*, as "a handsome, modern, wide-fronted house, with a big balcony before the drawing-room windows, and a flight of white marble steps ascending to a portal . . ."

There were no dormitory rooms for students when Parsons entered NYU in October 1844, and a university rule required that "Students whose parents reside in the city are supposed to live in their own families." For more than two years he lived with his mother and siblings at 15 Clifton Place, which was only a few blocks from the university. When their town house was sold during his junior year, he roomed nearby in a house on Eighth Street owned by a widowed friend of his mother, Mrs. Charles Jesup. A great benefit of the lodging arrangement for Parsons was the close and lasting friendship he developed with her son, Morris Ketchum Jesup, who became a railroad financier, philanthropist and first president of the American Museum of Natural History.

Both homes were close to the University Place Presbyterian Church, which Parsons regularly attended when he was not visiting his family in Rye. If he was feeling less pious, he could enjoy performances of opera and theater at the nearby Astor Place Opera House, which opened in November 1847 with a performance of Verdi's *Ernani*. Although he could not afford tickets to the expensive sections with upholstered seats, there were many seats available on benches that he could afford often enough to become a lifelong lover of opera.

Although he was fortunate to live in one of the more fashionable residential neighborhoods of New York, the rough and tumble sections of Five Points and the Bowery were not far away. That was made all too clear by the riot that occurred at the Astor Place Opera House on the night of May 10, 1849. It began when members of the Bowery Boys and other gangs of hooligans filled the galleries and, because of their nationalistic prejudices, broke up a performance of *Macbeth* by an English actor, W. C. Macready.

Outside the opera house, paving stones were thrown at police; the militia arrived; shots were fired and before the riot was over, twenty-two people had been killed. Although the event happened a year after Parsons graduated, the social and cultural forces that triggered it were part of a real-life education that students could find beyond the ivy-covered walls of NYU. Fortunately, Parsons managed to strike a good balance between the distractions of the city and the demands of his courses.

To gain admission to NYU, Parsons had to pass examinations in English grammar, geography, elements of history, arithmetic and algebra (through simple equations), *Caesar's Commentaries*, Virgil's *Aeneid, The Orations of Marcus Tillius Cicero*, Sallust, Greek New Testament, Xenophon's *Cycropaedia* and Homer's *Iliad*. It was a demanding set of requirements for such a young scholar, but the training he received at Samuel Berrian's school prepared him well to handle the academic challenges.

During freshman year, students were required to recite daily in Latin, Greek and mathematics, which appear from comments in his student diary to have been among Parsons's favorite classes along with upper-class courses in intellectual philosophy, history and belle-lettres. His study of political economy (the original name for the subject of economics) helped shape his later views as one of the country's leading business lawyers and antitrust experts.

The faculty included seven full-time professors and several part-time instructors, including Samuel F. B. Morse, who gave a course called Literature of the Arts of Design. Lectures and recitations occurred only in the mornings, leaving the afternoons and evenings free for students to study and socialize. There were no organized sports programs so the main extra-curricular activities revolved around the student-run societies and fraternities.

In the early part of the nineteenth century many colleges encouraged the formation of literary and debating societies on their campuses (often with Greek names) to promote both intellectual development and competitive school spirit. Princeton had the American Whig and Cliosophic societies, while at Columbia they were called the Philolexian and Peithologian societies. At NYU, there was a choice between the Eucleian and Philomathean societies.

Parsons decided to join the Philomathean Society, which occupied a room on the fourth floor of the University Building with its own library where the members held small meetings. Larger events, including debates and musical recitals, were held in the NYU chapel or the University Place Church. One of the notable participants in the Philomathean programs was Edgar Allan Poe, who lived near the university on Greenwich Street in the 1840s.

While he devoted much of his spare time to Philomathean affairs (serving as president for one term in his senior year), Parsons was also active in the Sigma Phi Society, a fraternity and secret society which originated at Union College in 1827. It was followed by the formation of sister chapters at Hamilton College, NYU, and on numerous other campuses.

Over the years, Parsons maintained close ties with a number of his fraternity brothers, especially his good friend, Elihu Root, a leading lawyer in New York, who became a United States senator, served as both secretary of war and secretary of state under President Theodore Roosevelt, and won the Nobel Peace Prize.

The college's finances and governance strengthened under the sound leadership of Theodore Frelinghuysen, who was appointed Chancellor in 1839 after James Matthews was forced to resign. Frelinghuysen was a distinguished lawyer and Presbyterian layman, who had served as U.S. senator from New Jersey from 1829 to 1835. In 1844 he was nominated to run for vice president on the Whig Party ticket, headed by Henry Clay. When James K. Polk and the Democratic Party won the election, NYU was spared the loss of its Chancellor.

During Parsons's years at NYU, the number of undergraduates grew from 131 to 153. The relatively small size of the student body gave Chancellor Frelinghuysen an opportunity to know a number of the undergraduates personally, especially those in classes he taught when the regular instructor was absent. Parsons's diary notes that on several occasions he "recited to the Chancellor," in a course called "Evidences of Revealed Religion." Even though NYU was non-sectarian, it was very much a Christian institution, requiring chapel attendance each morning before classes began.

Having acquired the habit of church-going from his devout Presbyterian grandfather, Parsons not only attended NYU chapel services during the week but also worshipped at the University Place Presbyterian Church twice on many Sundays. Throughout his adult life he played a leading role in various Protestant religious organizations, perhaps influenced by Chancellor Frelinghuysen, who was president of both the American Bible Society and the American Tract Society while he was at NYU.

The demands of his studies and frequent church attendance as well as his commitments to the Philomathean and Sigma Phi societies seemed all-consuming. Yet Parsons managed to find enough extra time to enjoy reading novels for pleasure and exploring New York City in search of useful, interesting and amusing diversions from the halls of NYU, as indicated by these excerpts from his diary, which were published in a 1954 issue of the *New-York Historical Society Quarterly*:

READING

Read "Nicholas Nickleby" [a story by Charles Dickens of a young man who has to support his mother and sister after his father dies that must have resonated strongly with John].

Commenced the "The Antiquary" [a gothic novel by Sir Walter Scott. In one week he read three other novels by Scott].

Read "Ten Thousand a Year" [written by an English barrister, Samuel Warren, whose commentary on details of the Common Law may have helped to spark Parsons's interest in a legal career. In senior year, he took a course that required reading Joseph Story's *Commentaries on the Constitution of the United States*].

Read the first volume of "Gil Blas" [a novel by Alain-René Lesage that depicts a young man who rises through the social and professional ranks through his wits and connections and retires to a castle, similar in many respects to John's own later life].

Read "Ernest Multravers" *& the sequel* "Alice" [by Sir Edward Bulwer-Lytton] *and vowed to give up reading novels* [but he kept up his voracious reading].

Stayed up till 12 reading the "Quiet Husband" [a novel by Elizabeth Pickering, an English writer of light novels].

Got Omoo, *also* Typee [both by Herman Melville, published in 1847 and 1846, respectively].

Samuel Berrian corresponded with Parsons about his studies, sending him a lengthy scolia or commentary in Greek on the *Medea* of Euripides on January 2, 1846. In a postscript he added: "My dear child, it does not sound well to hear that you are so fond of light reading, and I am half glad to hear that Prof. Lewis punished you for it, making you work harder on your Euripides."

EXERCISE AND RECREATION

Chopped wood and walked for exercise [he maintained his love of country life at his homes in Rye and Lenox, Massachusetts, until his death].

Dr. Henry not there the first hour: spent in snowballing. It snowed all day pretty fast making good sleighing.

Went round to the University . . . and then took the stage for 86th St. Borrowed . . . a pair of skates and went to a pond, a large though very rough pond. They were cutting ice out and while I was skating very fast over the bumps, looking up I saw myself not three feet from the hole. I couldn't stop so I kept on very fast and nearly cleared the hole (6 ft.). Went in about up to my armpits and came out wringing [he caught a bad cold afterwards].

At 4 AM got up and went for a horseback ride [he still rode when he was in his seventies, especially at his farm in Lenox].

Walked out to the new rail-depot [walking remained one of his passions, and on this occasion he walked more than twenty-five blocks up to the New York and Harlem railroad station at Thirty-second Street].

Went round to the Society in the evening but quickly returned to play chess with Morris [Jesup].

In the evening Captain Ottinger was here to tell me to be ready at 1 tomorrow to take a cruise in the Taney with the Russian Consul General. [Captain Douglass Ottinger was a U.S. Coast Guard officer who is credited with building the first life-saving stations on the Atlantic coast and may have been a family friend. They sailed for a week on Long Island Sound].

CULTURE

Went down to the Gallery of Fine Arts in the afternoon [he continued his interest in art as a collector and patron in later years].

In the evening went to the American Museum but was little pleased. [P.T. Barnum opened this museum in 1842 and ran it as a combination of zoo, waxworks, museum, theater and freak show].

To the [National] Academy of Design where I bought a season ticket and stayed a couple of hours [founded in 1825 by a group of artists including Samuel F. B. Morse].

In the evening to see Christy's Minstrels [a popular blackface group], *which pleased us very much.*

In the evening we all went round to the tabernacle to hear the Juvenile Oratorio Flora's Festival. Much pleased with the Hutchinsons. I believe we concluded the entertainment with some fine ballads [he continued to love vocal music and for many years was a box holder at the Metropolitan Opera].

SOCIAL AND PERSONAL

Went over to Hadden's to order a coat and vest for Mrs. Smith's blow out [several diary entries indicate his interest in clothes].

In the evening went to Mrs. Smith's party. Did not dance and enjoyed myself but little. About 150 to 200 there. Splendid supper [he also mentions enjoying new peas and strawberries when they came into season, and later in life he grew prize-winning vegetables at his Lenox farm].

At night before bedtime bathed my eyes in brandy and took an inward application also but they closed in the night [only mention of his drinking alcohol].

Received no valentines and wrote none.

Spent the evening most delightfully with her [no other information appears about "her" in the diary].

In June, 1848, Parsons graduated from NYU with a Bachelor of Arts degree and was chosen to give a commencement address as the English Salutatorian in a ceremony held at the University Place

Presbyterian Church. One of the youngest members of his class, he graduated third in academic ranking and was awarded the top prize in mathematics. Unfortunately, Ebenezer Clark was not on hand to see his grandson receive his university degree, as he had died the previous September.

In 1851, Parsons received an AM degree from NYU (as well as an honorary AM from Yale the same year). He was a frequent lecturer at the NYU law school and for thirty-three years (1865–1898) served as a member of the council of the university. The introduction to the published edition of Parsons's student diary notes, "This young graduate never really left the university as his loyalty was to constantly show itself officially and unofficially, through his long life."

Though his college years in Gotham had been a great success, Parsons had yet to experience much of the wider world. As a young boy, he once wrote his mother of his desire to see "the great world we live on." In 1852, he realized that goal when he took an extended trip to Washington, Charleston and Cuba, returning to New York via New Orleans and along the Mississippi and Ohio Rivers. Some of the excerpts from the journal he kept of the journey provide interesting insights into his views as a young adult:

> When we are always kept in one place our thoughts seem unable to pass a certain compass, and as we enlarge the objects for our thoughts . . . we make them the fertile soil in which ideas are ever springing up. I have been particularly fastened to my home by my position as head of our family and by that love of our dear mother . . .

Delaware is by far the finest land I have seen since leaving NY . . . the farms appear neat [and] are usually cultivated by slave labor. It is here that I made my first acquaintance with the peculiar institution of the south. The farmers are careless and improvident and their negroes are being rapidly sold to the South to pay the debts of their extravagant masters . . .

The Capitol [in Washington] and its grounds are adorned with paintings and statuary . . . a historical painting which is designed chiefly to preserve national portraits . . . is seldom pleasing as a painting. Still, the associations connected with such scenes, and the thoughts that cluster around them inflame even my cold blood and make me glow with a patriotic pride . . . [his favorite painting is the *Embarkation of the Pilgrims* by Robert Weir]

It is a noble sight to see the pride of European soldiers and the haughtiness of European aristocracy humbled before [those] who in their devotion to grand and universal principles of right were invincible before their enemies. Happy will we be as a nation if we follow the glorious example which they have set for us and go on in this road which they have opened . . .

There is seen here [North Carolina] none of those objects which lend so great a charm to those shores and hills of New England. No pretty white houses and neat yards here tell of comfort and happiness—no village spires ever point up to heaven—there is no activity—I very much mistake if slavery is not the root and mother of all this . . . slavery is the bane of the earth, sinking the masters fast into that degradation which must result from so close intercourse and communion with those they have so much degraded . . .

We do not enjoy things half so much as we would if we had some ear to tell our enjoyment . . . you particularly desire and need a lady friend to accompany you. After being confined to the company of your own sex for a while, you get barbarous, selfish, ill-mannered and lose all that polish and considerate feeling, which communion with women gives and strengthens.

Steam has annihilated space and we measure distance now in time. We leave Charleston . . . and arrive here [Havana] after a voyage of 76 hours. I have made almost my first experience of the sea, and with disappointment I love the water . . . in its storms and calm . . . [despite the tragic drowning of his father in the shipwreck].

In fact, the ladies of Havana are hidden in real Spanish seclusion, and can only be seen behind the curtains of a volante, at church or at the opera. There seems to be little need of this imprisonment, as the women I have seen have been almost without exception not only not pretty, but ugly. They have always bright eyes, with no softness of expression, dark complexion and hair and awkward figures . . . but [there was] one whom I thought was beautiful, and her face has haunted me ever since . . . I like their dress generally, which is far more modest than that of our ladies at home—not so much exposure of person.

At the NYU graduation ceremonies four years before, Parsons and his classmates had a somewhat less conservative view of their ideal woman when they sang:

But now New York I leave, sir,
To breast the waves of life.
I'm going to serve my country
And sport a pretty wife . . .

With the Mexican War behind them and the Civil War not yet on the horizon, the graduates of the class of 1848 had reason to be quite optimistic about their futures.

Chapter Four

Success in the Law

Only eighteen when he graduated from NYU, Parsons later recalled: "What was to be my occupation in life had remained in abeyance. My choice inclined to be a banker as furnishing the opportunity most quickly of making a fortune [but] no opportunity came . . . In the autumn of 1848 I determined to try the law, although with no very definite purpose to become a lawyer, if an opportunity offered of being employed in a banker's office."

He once told a group of lawyers that he had first considered becoming a lawyer in his youth when he visited the Jay family burial ground that bordered his family's property in Rye: "As I stood in front of the square monument erected to the memory of John Jay, the first Chief Justice of the United States; distinguished as a lawyer and as a statesman and, looking at that stone and having in mind the memory of that man, I found some temptation to become a member of that profession which he considered so illustrious . . ."

Because of his ambivalence about a legal career, Parsons had no incentive to enroll in one of the few law schools that then existed. Harvard and Yale had opened law schools in 1817 and 1826, respectively, followed by NYU in 1835 and Columbia in 1858. According to

John E. Parsons outwitting opposing counsel (cartoon courtesy of David Parsons)

Theodore Dwight, Columbia's first law school dean, when the school was founded, "it was considered at that time mainly as an experiment . . . Most of the leading lawyers had obtained their training in offices or by private reading, and were highly skeptical as to the possibility of securing competent legal knowledge by means of professional schools."

Therefore, Parsons followed the path taken by most of those who aspired to enter the legal profession—by serving as clerks to practicing attorneys before passing examinations that qualified them to be admitted to the bar. Prior to 1847, admission to the New York State bar required several exams and could take up to ten years for someone to qualify, first as an attorney, then as solicitor and finally as a counsellor. Amendments to the state constitution in 1847 eliminated distinctions between categories of lawyers and allowed any man (no women were then lawyers) over twenty-one with "requisite qualifications" to practice at all levels of the state's courts.

Despite the easier licensing requirements and proliferation of lawyers, growth of banking and commerce in New York City attracted many talented attorneys, most of whom practiced individually or in small firms. Through his uncle, James Hewitt, Parsons was fortunate to obtain a clerkship with the establishment firm of Gerard & Platt, whose office at 79 Nassau Street was in the heart of New York's business and financial district.

An article in *Frank Leslie's Popular Monthly* painted a Dickensian picture of what a young law clerk in a New York firm faced in the days just prior to the Civil War: "The offices, the paraphernalia, the methods of drawing papers, the details of practice, all were simplicity itself . . . Wooden or cane-bottom chairs, oilcloth-covered tables, pine bookcases, old-fashioned foolscap on which to draw pleadings . . . The solitary clerk . . . kept the books for his chief on the munificent salary of five dollars per week . . ."

By taking notes for James Gerard in the court room, Parsons was able to observe the styles and tactics of various trial lawyers. A favorite and winning tactic of Gerard, according to Parsons, was to "take a seat as near as was possible to the jury, establish personal relations with them, and conduct the trial in a conversational way until there was such a feeling and sympathy between Gerard and the jury that he had won the trial before the summing up." He later told a graduating class at NYU Law School that Gerard liked to say that the quality that made a lawyer successful was "spontaneous combustion."

While Gerard was a successful litigator, his partner James Platt was, in Parsons's view, "better versed in the law than any lawyer whom I have known." Because Platt had injured his eyes, Parsons read the reports of cases to him and heard his instructive comments. A great friend of Parsons's, Joseph Choate, once said of that early legal training: "He went back to the reports, the real embodiment of the existing law, and mastered them individually in the same way as they were subsequently used collectively under the system that bears the name of Professor Langdell [who introduced the case method at Harvard Law School]."

During his clerkship with Gerard & Platt, one of their clients got him interested in a venture to build a canal in Nicaragua. As he later confessed, "there came a time when [the client] was expected to return from Europe with important concessions. The shares began to advance. I put all that I had in them; it turned out the concessions were not obtained, so I was made to realize that I had to work for a living."

After spending two years in his first clerkship, Parsons moved to the firm of Benedict & Boardman where he broadened his legal education and also improved his pay, first to six and then to eight dollars per week. The training he received from Andrew Boardman in real estate law provided a solid foundation for his later expertise in that area of the law. In a landmark case (*Dunham v. Williams*) decided in 1867, Parsons convinced New York's highest court to apply the civil law of the Netherlands rather than the common law rule in deciding title to the bed of a road that dated back to the Dutch colonial period in New York.

Parsons also had a valuable role model in Charles O'Conor, a partner in Benedict & Boardman who had won a high-profile divorce case, representing the wife of Edwin Forrest, one of the best-known actors in the country. When Forrest died in 1872, eight years after the divorce became final, Parsons was then one of the lawyers who obtained a large award of unpaid alimony for Forrest's ex-wife.

Recognizing that the Forrest case had helped to establish O'Conor's position as "perhaps the ablest member of our Bar," Parsons went on to represent a number of clients in celebrated divorce cases during his long career. One of the most contentious and protracted of these was the De Meli divorce suit that was tried over many months, beginning in June 1883. Parsons represented Mrs. Florence De Meli, who charged her husband, Henry, with cruelty. He, in turn, counter-claimed for divorce on the grounds of adultery and desertion.

After Mrs. De Meli fled their home in Dresden, Germany, to escape his abuse, her husband obtained a German divorce, which the New York courts ruled was invalid. He brought witnesses from a German spa to give evidence of her infidelity. The newspapers had a field day, with one *Times* article carrying the headlines "Horrid Girls Who Carried on with Her Husband—Baron Von Geyso's Playful Letters—Mr. De Meli Accompanied by His Female Cook on His Travels."

As reported by the *Times,* the normally dispassionate Parsons pulled out the stops in his summary statement, asking the jury: "Shall the result of this suit be that Mrs. De Meli shall be driven from this court an outcast, her character gone, a thing to be pointed at with scorn; that she shall be deprived of her children and the recognition of her friends forever? Shall she be compelled to return to a man who [is] a beer-drinking, child-beating, euchre-playing, absinthe-sipping, staggerer through the streets?"

The judge found that, under New York law, there had to be actual evidence of physical abuse to grant the plaintiff a divorce on the grounds of cruelty, but he also found that there was insufficient evidence of adultery to support the defendant's cross-suit for divorce. He also ruled that Mr. De Meli had to reimburse his wife for her legal costs, including $500 for Parsons's attorney fees. The case, however, continued through two appeals and was not resolved until 1890 when the New York Court of Appeals upheld all of the trial judge's rulings, leaving Mr. and Mrs. De Meli unhappily married (under New York law) until the husband's death in 1915.

When his client in another divorce case was the husband, Parsons told the jury in his opening remarks, "I am here in discharge of the highest duty to which a lawyer is called—to preserve the home; to prevent it from bursting asunder of the sacred relation of the husband and wife; to prevent those innocent children from going forth into the world without the care of a father, without a share in his fortune . . ." The case was decided in favor of his wealthy client.

After he was admitted to the bar in 1852, Parsons was offered a junior partnership by Benedict & Boardman, but he decided to strike out on his own. His uncle James gave him space in his office at the corner of William and Pine Streets where he hung out his shingle. He recalled that for quite a while his only clients were "members of my family, and one or two persons of little importance whom I advised on mortgage investments."

Fortunately, his career took a leap upward when a friend from NYU introduced Parsons to a successful young lawyer, Lorenzo B. Shepard, who invited him to become his partner. Within months of forming the firm of Shepard & Parsons in 1854, the New York County District Attorney died in the wreck of the steamship *Arctic*, which sank after a collision in the north Atlantic with the loss of more than 300 lives.

Lorenzo Shepard was appointed to fill the vacancy, and, shortly afterward, Parsons was surprised to find on his desk a letter from Shepard that read: "Dear Sir, I have the honor to inform you that I have been appointed by his Excellency, Horatio Seymour, Governor of the State, to be District Attorney of this County, and I hereby appoint you to be my assistant." Parsons went next door into Shepard's office, and protested that he did not know anything about criminal law, to which Shepard replied, "It is very important that you learn as quickly as you can."

After agreeing to serve as Shepard's sole assistant district attorney, Parsons spent seven months preparing all the indictments and prosecuting almost all of the cases. Toward the end of his career, Parsons wrote later in a diary that "I have always considered this experience as a principal factor in contributing to such success as later came to me as a court lawyer."

When their brief sojourn in the District Attorney's office ended, Shepard and Parsons resumed their private law practice, but Shepard, who had become increasingly active in Democratic politics, was elected New York City's Corporation Counsel in 1855. He also was made "Grand Sachem" (head) of the political organization known as Tammany Hall, replacing Fernando Wood who was elected to his first term as Mayor of New York that year.

Shepard remained his nominal partner, but Parsons, who operated the firm essentially by himself, managed to develop a number of new clients. Among them were Peter Cooper, (the noted inventor and philanthropist) as well as his son Edward and son-in-law, Abram Hewitt (both future mayors of New York City), all of whom would play important roles in Parsons's life.

His law practice was beginning to flourish when Lorenzo Shepard died suddenly at the age of thirty-six in September of 1856. Within only a few months, however, Albon P. Man, one of the most respected business lawyers in New York, invited him to become a partner in the firm of Edwards and Man. The partnership became Man and Parsons in 1863 when Edwards retired, and lasted until 1884.

Among the talented young lawyers who were students and clerks at the firm was Edward M. Shepard, a son of Lorenzo Shepard, who later became a partner of Parsons. For a brief period in the 1860s, the firm also employed a bright young law clerk named Elihu Root, a recent graduate of NYU Law School, who later became a close friend and colleague of Parsons.

In 1913, when Root was serving a U.S. senator from New York, he wrote Parsons: "It is hard to realize what a change in elevators and stenographers and typewriters and telephones have made. I don't know of any better law offices now or any more workmanlike or effective argument or trial of causes of any sounder law that could be found in the office of Man and Parsons in the year 1867."

Included among the firm's clients were many wealthy New York families whose business interests and estates often involved lawsuits that required Parsons's courtroom skills. Another lawyer who was a clerk at the firm later reported that he reviewed some seventy cases that had been tried by Parsons and found that he had succeeded in every trial as well as with those he argued on appeal.

In one case, he represented a woman whose previous lawyers had failed to win her a share of her father's estate in a prolonged legal fight with her brother. A newspaper account of the trial, describing the questioning of the brother by Parsons, said that the witness "had to endure a fire of questions, which many men of means would give a tidy sum to avoid." The court's finding that the plaintiff was entitled to one-third of the estate was credited by the newspaper largely to the skills of Parsons in cross-examining witnesses.

Occasionally, however, he was on the losing side, especially when he had to defend a hopeless cause. That was the case when the tobacco company tycoon and sportsman, Pierre Lorillard, instead of settling, was sued for $40,000 in damages because of necessary repairs to a leaky yacht he had sold to a Wall Street banker. Although he lost the case, Parsons had the pleasure of sparring in the court room with his great friend and frequent adversary, Joseph Choate, including these exchanges that appeared in the *Times*:

"I object to that," said Mr. Parsons. "I must protect Mr. Lorillard from these affidavits."

"I agree with Mr. Parsons on that," answered Mr. Choate, "that 'poor Mr. Lorillard,' as he has been called, needs protection."

"Even if he is rich Mr. Lorillard, he still needs protection," retorted Mr. Parsons. After Lorillard had finished being questioned by Choate, he sat down and whispered something laughingly to Parsons, who said to Choate,

"Mr. Lorillard wants to know if you don't think he's a good witness."

"Very good, very good, indeed," replied Mr. Choate. "It's the first time he's ever been examined as a witness," said Mr. Parsons, "so you've had a virgin opportunity."

There were numerous other cases that brought Parsons and Choate together in the court room, usually on opposite sides. Newspapers and magazines delighted in capturing and reporting their witty ripostes, including one widely quoted exchange during a trial in a Westchester County court in which Parsons, who had a home in the county, cautioned the jury not to be swayed by "Mr. Choate's Chesterfieldian urbanity." To which Choate retorted that his style could not match the "Westchesterfieldian suburbanity" of Parsons.

When the two legal lions faced off in an 1898 case, a *Times* article reported that "Mr. Choate severely handled Mr. W. H. Hurlburt, a witness for the will." According to the *Times* reporter, when it was time for Parsons to interrogate Hurlburt (his client), he began: "Mr. Choate having frequently sneered at you as a 'Yale man'—he being a Harvard man." Choate promptly moved to strike that statement, adding, "I never sneer."

Speaking at a birthday dinner for Parsons in 1914, Choate said, "I always admired one great trait of his, which has been the secret of his success, and that was his absolute self-control. No matter what happened, in any controversy in which we were engaged, he never lost his self-control." Choate must have missed a session in the famous Fayerweather will contest when Parsons became so aggravated at one of the opposing counsel that he told him: "Never speak to me again, in or out of court."

Parsons had to face this nemesis, William Blaikie, in another court room battle in 1901. Blaikie represented plaintiffs who sued Parsons's firm, claiming that it had collected too much in fees from a settlement it had won on their behalf. The *Times* reported that "These two lawyers were arrayed against each other in the *Fayerweather* will contest and fought each legal point very bitterly. The same legal fencing has developed in the present action."

During a trial in 1877, Parsons's opponent was a distinguished older lawyer, Joshua Van Cott. According to a report in the *Brooklyn Eagle*, after Parsons completed his presentation of the case, Van Cott said in his opening statement: "I never rise to answer my friend in an important case without a feeling of oppression. He is a great artist in the construction of evidence and also in the construction of a case, and his gifts in that line excite in my breast apprehensions of the impression he is producing."

At the 1914 birthday dinner for Parsons, Joseph Choate told the gathering: "My recollection of Mr. Parsons dates back nearly fifty years, and during that time . . . we have been very closely united in the bonds of friendship and the bonds of hostility. We have been fighting as well as we could all the time, and I do not know which got the better of it. We took very different views of life and of the business of lawsuits. I thought the great object of a lawsuit was to get all the fun out of it I could, and I generally succeeded; and Mr. Parsons thought that the object was to perform a stern and serious duty to his conscience and his clients."

Parsons believed he owed a serious duty to his clients even when their activities were scandalous, as occurred when he represented a man in a child custody battle. Reporting on the judge's decision, the *Times* noted that "the father became acquainted with the mother in an assignation house, and the child was born of illicit intercourse." Parsons won an award of custody for his client by proving that the mother was then keeping a house of prostitution.

In a series of complex trials and investigative hearings over many years, Parsons skillfully defended one of his more colorful clients, Theodore Davis, who managed to avoid disbarment and even jail for alleged fraud and perjury. After amassing a fortune from successful investments in speculative ventures, Davis purchased a large mansion in Newport and became a respected archeologist in Egypt's Valley of the Kings. In representing clients like Davis, Parsons recognized that he, as a lawyer, had to weigh the reputational risk against both his duty to the client as well the financial rewards.

As his reputation for winning cases grew, Parsons's courtroom appearances often received wide coverage by newspapers in New York and elsewhere in the country. None, however, received more attention than the case brought in 1888 by Clara Campbell, an aspiring opera singer, against Charles Arbuckle, a millionaire coffee merchant. The plaintiff, described by one reporter, as "somewhat beyond her prime" sued Parsons's client for breach of promise of marriage, claiming damages of $250,000.

The plaintiff's evidence included letters between the couple, signed "Bunnie" (Campbell) and "Baby Bunting" (Arbuckle) that became the talk of the town, if not the entire country. The *Times* reported that "Miss Campbell was on the stand during the entire day, and Mr. Parsons was as studiously and politely provoking as usual in his cross-examination."

The *Times* reporter, who was obviously a close observer of Parsons's courtroom style, noted that Miss Campbell revealed "she has a temper of her own, which Mr. Parsons was glad to discover." However, "she has it under the completest kind of subjection, which was not so pleasing to the defendant's leading counsel, whose most brilliant achievements are accomplished when he provokes a witness to anger by force of his own exasperating serenity."

It is curious that Arbuckle and Campbell did not settle their dispute out of court and thereby avoid the humiliation that resulted from the trial publicity. Even though Parsons did not win a verdict for his client, he managed to persuade the jury to award "Bunnie" only $45,000, less than one-fifth the amount she sought. It was not until 1935 that the New York State legislature passed a law that abolished the cause of action for damages based on a breach of promise to marry.

In one of his few criminal cases, Parsons headed a team of experienced trial lawyers who defended a well-known New York businessman named Jacob Sharp, who was described in the newspapers both as a "boodler" and "a gentleman of colossal infamy." Sharp was accused of bribing a city alderman to support his bid for a valuable surface railroad franchise along Broadway, a prize he had been attempting to win for many years.

The *Times* report of the trial referred to Sharp's counsel team as "those eminent gentlemen and upright citizens, who, presumably through their belief that he has been wrongfully accused, have contracted to use all their talent and energies to assist Mr. Sharp in escaping punishment."

Parsons opened the case for the defense with an address to the jury that lasted more than four hours, but, according to the *Times*, he "never lost their attention." The trial lasted five weeks and, despite the efforts of Parsons and his co-counsel, the jury returned a verdict of guilty. The judge then sentenced Sharp to four years in the penitentiary at Sing Sing.

The defense lawyers expedited an appeal all the way to the Court of Appeals, which reversed the verdict of the trial judge, based on errors in his admission of evidence, and granted a new trial. When Jacob Sharp died before a new trial began, articles carrying details of the case appeared in newspapers all over the country (e.g. *The Omaha Bee*: "Jake Sharp, King of the New York Boodlers Expires").

Interest in the case was generated not only by evidence of New York official corruption but also by concerns about judicial due process and public fairness. It was not just his family and lawyers who would have agreed with the headline in the Springfield, Ohio, *Daily Republic* that Sharp was "at last beyond the reach of courts and newspapers." Memories of the case lingered a long time.

When one of the appellate judges, Joseph Potter, died nearly twenty years later, the *New York Tribune* noted that, "The most conspicuous act of Judge Potter's successful judicial career was the granting of a stay of proceedings in the case of Jacob Sharp, who was convicted of bribery . . . He granted the stay despite the strong opposition of many of the public . . ."

Beginning in the 1870s, competition between New York's surface and elevated railways was fierce, resulting in numerous lawsuits that provided lucrative business for Parsons and other lawyers. Adding to the conflicts was a law (the Street Railway Act) that required approval of new lines from owners of at least half of the value of property along the proposed line.

Representing owners of property along Third Avenue, Parsons spent years in hearings before transit commissioners, followed by trials and appeals in the lower courts before the Court of Appeals finally ruled for his clients in 1882. One newspaper noted that "This decision (*Story v. New York Elevated R.R. Co.*) is one of the most important ever handed down by a court in this state."

That decision spawned a multitude of other elevated railroad cases, which brought considerable fame and financial success to Parsons and other lawyers in the following years. According to an article in an 1893 issue of the *Yale Law Journal*, more than two thousand such cases were constantly pending, with millions of dollars of damages (not to mention attorneys' fees) at stake. It was a major battle between the interests of private property and small business owners and those of developers, entrepreneurs and capitalists.

The *Story* case was only one of nearly 150 cases Parsons argued before New York's Court of Appeals, in addition to the more than 30 cases in which he represented clients before the U.S. Supreme Court. Even though he still tried cases and handled appeals well into his seventies, he, like other leading lawyers of his time, increasingly was retained to advise clients in his office rather than to represent them as an advocate in the courtroom.

Speaking at a memorial service in 1902 for his friend and fellow lawyer, William Allen Butler, Parsons might have been describing his own legal career when he said: "Mr. Butler was too sound and sagacious an adviser in his office, too brilliant and successful an advocate in the courts to devote himself exclusively to one or the other of the two main divisions of the profession . . . Perhaps his most effective work was as an advocate, and especially in the appellate courts, where his deep knowledge of the law, his phenomenal memory, his remarkable powers of elucidation and illustration of legal principles, and his temperate and almost judicial attitude of mind, were most effectively brought into play . . ."

Chapter Five

Peter Cooper and His Union

When Parsons died in 1915, his obituary in the *New York Times* noted: "It is said that it was Mr. Parsons's custom to give from one-quarter to one half of his income each year to charity." Over his long life Parsons contributed generously to numerous charitable and civic organizations, but he supported them as much through his legal and leadership talents as with his substantial wealth.

He followed the example of his civic-minded and philanthropic grandfather, Ebenezer Clark, who was a pillar of the Presbyterian Church and the community of Rye. No one influenced Parsons more in his adult life, however, than Peter Cooper, who used his financial success as an inventor and manufacturer to become one of the most prominent philanthropists and civic leaders in nineteenth-century New York City.

Andrew Carnegie could have been speaking for both Parsons and himself when he said of Peter Cooper at a dinner in 1909 (at which Parsons presided): "He was my great exemplar, one in whose footsteps I humbly try to tread. For he was a believer in the idea that wealth is a sacred trust, the surplus to be distributed during one's lifetime for the benefit of our fellow-men . . . and he thought, as I have thought,

View of Cooper Union, circa 1861 (courtesy of New York Public Library)

that in encouraging and aiding education, wealth can be employed to great good."

Cooper was the epitome of an entrepreneur, combining a talent for invention with managerial abilities that made him successful in various business and real estate ventures during his long life (1791–1883). He turned the mundane manufacture of glue into a highly profitable enterprise and multiplied his earnings by investing in iron mines, foundries and rolling mills. Of all his business successes, perhaps the best-known were his design of the first American-built steam locomotive, called the "Tom Thumb" (because of its small size) and the completion of the first transatlantic telegraph cable in which he was a major investor.

He is best remembered, however, for founding the Cooper Union for the Advancement of Science and Art as a tuition-free institution of higher learning. From the outset, it enrolled both male and female students from the working classes without regard to race or religious affiliation. He had conceived the idea thirty years earlier while serving as a New York City Alderman and began to develop the plan for it, inspired by the success of a polytechnic school in Paris.

The cornerstone of Cooper Union was laid in 1853 by Peter Cooper and Mayor William Havemeyer, but it took another six years and nearly $700,000 to complete the original building, in addition to the land acquisition costs. There were many obstacles to overcome, including the Panic of 1857, which caused construction delays and required Cooper to sell some securities to provide additional funds. To assure that his plan started on a sound legal basis Cooper turned to his young lawyer, John E. Parsons, who was under thirty years old when Cooper became his client.

Parsons had impressed Cooper with the handling of a lawsuit against heirs of Peter Stuyvesant in which the Court of Appeals ruled that New York City could create a public square on Stuyvesant property near Cooper Union. That case called for knowledge of New York real property law, but his next project for Cooper required expertise in the laws governing corporations, nonprofit organizations, taxation and trusts.

Like any good lawyer, Parsons did some careful research. Nonprofit educational institutions had existed in America since the founding of Harvard in 1638. Typically, they had no owners or stockholders, were governed by a board of trustees and could accept charitable donations and bequests for their educational purposes. In the early years after the founding of the Republic, however, many states actively promoted public over private institutions.

These political conflicts came to a head in the famous Dartmouth College case, decided by the U.S. Supreme Court in 1819. The court ruled that the State of New Hampshire had violated the contracts clause of the U.S. Constitution in taking over a privately endowed college. The decision, therefore, assured future donors, like Cooper, that the institutions they founded and supported would be free of government interference with valid contracts.

With the Dartmouth case as background, Parsons prepared a deed of trust in April 1859 by which Peter Cooper and his wife donated the building and other property to a board of trustees for the benefit of Cooper Union. In that same month, the New York State Legislature passed a law granting a corporate charter to Cooper Union, which referred to the Cooper gift. A key clause of the statute and charter provided:

"The premises and property mentioned in said deed, and which at any time shall belong to or be held in trust by the corporation hereby created, or by the trustees thereof, including all endowments made to it, shall not, nor shall any part thereof, be subject to taxation while the same shall be appropriated to the uses, intents and purposes hereby and in the said deed provided for."

The statutory exemption from taxation contained in the charter would prove highly beneficial over the years in realizing Cooper's goal of providing tuition-free education to students of Cooper Union. In a letter dated April 29, 1859, which accompanied the Deed of Trust, he explained: "In order to encourage the young to improve and better their condition, I have provided for a continued course of lectures, discussions and recitations in the most useful and practical sciences, to be open and free to all . . ."

Cooper imagined the institution not just as a college but as a "union" where the city's workers as well as their children could attend meetings and lectures as well as enroll in classes. Running both evening and daytime sessions, Cooper Union provided the first example of continuing education.

Cooper chose five men to serve with him on the initial board of trustees: his son, Edward Cooper, his son-in-law Abram Hewitt, Daniel F. Tiemann, Wilson G. Hunt and John E. Parsons. From the start there was strong political and business support for the school. Daniel Tiemann was mayor of New York when it opened, and Hewitt as well as the younger Cooper later were elected to that office. Other than Parsons, all of the trustees in the first fifty years were successful men of business or finance, including J. P. Morgan, Jr. and Andrew Carnegie.

On November 2, 1859, the Cooper Union for the Advancement

of Science and Art was formally inaugurated. At its opening, the wide choice of subjects included mathematics, philosophy, design, chemistry, architectural, mechanical and free-hand drawing, vocal music and debating. Among the early students was the sculptor Augustus Saint-Gaudens, who enrolled as an art student at the age of thirteen in 1861.

The Cooper "Institute," as it was known for many years was housed in an imposing six-story building erected at Astor Place between Third and Fourth Avenues. In addition to classrooms, the school's Foundation Building included a public reading room, stocked with the latest newspapers and periodicals, which was always filled with New Yorkers, whether or not they were enrolled as students. By the 1880s, it had a daily attendance of more than 1,500.

Another major attraction was the Great Hall in the basement of the building, which was for many years the largest meeting room in the city for free lectures as well as public meetings. Cooper chose to build the large auditorium in the basement for safety reasons, believing it could be evacuated in the case of fire more easily and with less risk of people being trampled.

Shortly after the building opened the Great Hall made history when Abraham Lincoln delivered a key speech there at the start of his campaign for the presidency in 1860. In what is known as his "Cooper Union Address," Lincoln concluded with the powerful challenge: "Let us have faith that right makes might, and in that faith, let us, to the end, dare to do our duty as we understand it."

With the growing conflict over slavery and the importance of the upcoming November presidential election, the address by a relatively unknown Abraham Lincoln drew an audience of more than 1,200 men and women to Cooper Union on the night of February 27. As

Lincoln scholar Harold Holzer describes the event, "At first, Lincoln's high-pitched voice grated, yet soon he settled into his rhythm. When he finished, the house broke out in wild and prolonged enthusiasm."

Along with Peter Cooper and the other trustees of Cooper Union, Parsons must have, in Holzer's words "marveled at the westerner's transformation from a countrified stump-speaker to a dignified states-man." None of the trustees was a Republican (Daniel Tiemann was then serving as mayor in a Democratic-coalition administration), but all were opposed to slavery. In February 1863, Frederick Douglass spoke at Cooper Union in praise of the Emancipation Proclamation, which President Lincoln had issued just weeks before.

While Peter Cooper remained president of Cooper Union until his death in 1883, Hewitt effectively headed the board in his role as secretary until his death in 1903. Edward Cooper assumed his father's role as president, but at his death in 1905 Parsons became both the actual and titular head of the board for the next ten years.

During a memorial gathering at Cooper Union held shortly after Parsons's death in 1915, Peter Cooper's granddaughter, Sarah Cooper Hewitt, described Parsons's nearly six decades of service as a Cooper Union trustee:

"In 1859 . . . Mr. Parsons was a brilliant young lawyer . . . but so comparatively unknown that he often related how profoundly sur-prised, touched and honored he felt that Mr. Cooper should have considered him worthy to share in the great and heavy task of serving as one of the five Trustees of his Foundation.

"Doubtless the deep and lifelong friendship that subsisted between him and Mr. Cooper arose in those early days when Mr. Par-sons, before his marriage, as well as my father [Abram Hewitt], also a bachelor, had rooms at Dr. Rawson's, just opposite my grandfather's house [at the corner of Lexington Avenue and Twenty-second Street].

"It is pleasant to picture those two enthusiastic and ambitious, remarkable young men, seated upon the high stoop of the older man, during the long spring and summer evenings, according to the charmingly simple old Dutch custom that still survived in New York at that time, while he eagerly unfolded to them all the details of his cherished plan and secured their advice and devoted cooperation."

In addition to his pro bono legal work for Cooper Union over many years, Parsons remained the personal lawyer for Peter Cooper and members of his family as well as their glue factory and other ventures. After Cooper lost badly in the presidential election of 1876, running as the candidate of the Greenback Party, he was sued for libel by a man he had accused of intentionally undermining his campaign.

The *Brooklyn Eagle* described the scene at the start of the trial in 1878: "The venerable Peter Cooper inflated his air cushion [his portable seat wherever he went] and eased himself into his seat in the Supreme Court, Brooklyn, drew a ladies fan from his pocket and fanned himself." As the trial dragged on, Cooper became agitated at some of the testimony of witnesses, and began raising his hand to object to various assertions, whereupon, according to the newspaper, "Mr. Parsons would seize it, draw down, saying 'keep still.' Then Mr. Cooper would shake his counsel's hand, saying, 'I will, I will.'" Eventually, Parsons was able to preserve the dignity of his venerable client (as well as saving him from paying damages of $50,000) when the trial ended with a jury verdict in favor of Cooper.

When Cooper died on April 4, 1883 at the age of 92, New York City mourned its First Citizen. After a private ceremony at his home, his funeral was held at All Souls' Unitarian Church where an estimated fifteen thousand people viewed his open coffin. Among the eminent pallbearers were former Governor Hamilton Fish and Cyrus Field, Cooper's partner in laying the first trans-Atlantic cable, as well as Parsons and the other non-family trustees of Cooper Union.

Following the ceremony, the coffin was placed in a horse-drawn hearse for its journey to Brooklyn. According to an account in the *New York Herald,* "Slowly at first, individual spectators solemnly began to fall in behind the cortege. Soon whole crowds of people spontaneously left the sidewalks and joined the procession until it was a vast river of silent humanity snaking its way through the streets of lower New York. At the ferry house, 'amid the whistling of the ferry-boats and the rattling of the elevated trains,' the funeral party boarded a ferry for the short trip to Brooklyn where he was buried in Greenwood Cemetery."

Shortly after Cooper's death, an article in the *Herald* described the impressive progress of Cooper Union since its opening in 1859. The article ended with praise for the management of Cooper Union's finances by the trustees, who had all served since the incorporation:

> It costs about $50,000 a year to run the institution, and it is practically self-supporting; the income being derived from the stores in the lower part of the building, the great hall in the basement and the interest on the founder's endowment fund. The expenditures by the Trustees on the building and education from 1859 to 1882, inclusive were only $1,549,192. Reckoning the thousands of pupils that have passed through its classes, and the hundreds of thousands that have benefitted by its other advantages of instruction, this comparatively

small sum spent in twenty-three years will appear a very economical means to very large and useful ends.

During his lifetime, Peter Cooper gave nearly $1,500,000 to Cooper Union and contributed an additional $200,000 in his will. Edward Cooper and the Hewitt family donated another $400,000 to pay for structural repairs to the building in the 1880s. Despite these gifts, the trustees decided to make an unprecedented appeal for donations from the public in the annual report of 1884. They cited the pressing need to enlarge the teaching area so more students could be admitted from the waiting list. Initially, this could be done by utilizing space rented to businesses, but income from increased endowment would then be needed to offset the lost rental income.

The response to the public appeals was slow in coming, but in the late 1890s major gifts were received from the estates of Peter Cooper's brother and sister. These were followed in the early 1900s by a bequest of $250,000 from financier Henry H. Rogers, a close friend of Hewitt, and another of $400,000 from John Halstead, a tea merchant who greatly admired what Cooper had done for education, although they had never met.

The largest and most significant of these donations came in two stages from Andrew Carnegie. In 1900, he gave $300,000 to establish a free polytechnic day school, completing Peter Cooper's original educational plan. In a letter to Abram Hewitt, Carnegie wrote: "As a humble follower of Peter Cooper, among the first of our disciples of the Gospel of Wealth, it would be a rare satisfaction indeed for me to be allowed to feel that I had contributed the last stone, as it were, to the cairn of his great benefaction."

When the gift was announced, an editorial in the *Times* praised Carnegie's generosity, commenting that "You cannot endow a great university by passing around the hat, and you cannot get Congress or the State Legislatures to appropriate millions for Cooper Unions . . ." Nonetheless, the trustees still faced a shortage of funds.

Two years later, Carnegie gave an additional $300,000, and his total gift of $600,000 was matched by an equal amount from a trust established by Peter Cooper for his children and grandchildren. The circumstances were recorded in the minutes of the Board of Trustees meeting on February 4, 1902: "In order, therefore, that Mr. Carnegie's second gift might be met by an equivalent from Mr. Cooper's family, they have agreed to convey property known as the Vanderbilt Flats, constituting the trust property above referred to, valued at six hundred thousand dollars . . ."

The minutes of that meeting also included the following resolution: "Resolved, that the Trustees express by this minute their appreciation of the beneficent action of Andrew Carnegie and of the filial action of the family of Mr. Cooper and Mr. Hewitt in thus carrying into effect the great purpose of Peter Cooper to found an institution for the free instruction and improvement of men and women engaged in occupations necessary for their support . . ."

At the time of the transfer, the property was occupied by what the *New York Times* described as "a monotonous looking row of five-story brownstone buildings on East Forty-third Street, known as the Vanderbilt Flats . . ." The income derived from this property and the Carnegie endowment added $30,000 per year, allowing Cooper Union both to cease renting out space in its building and to avoid charging tuition. This very complex transaction, crafted by Parsons as legal adviser for both the family and Cooper Union, would prove to be of enormous long-term benefit to Cooper Union.

When Cooper Union was not able to have the Vanderbilt Flats property removed from the New York City tax rolls in 1903, Parsons and his law firm challenged the tax assessment in the state courts. In a 1905 case known as *Cooper Union v. Wells*, the New York Court of Appeals held, without a written opinion, that it was illegal for the city to assess a tax on the property conveyed to Cooper Union as part of its endowment.

In effect, the Court of Appeals adopted the opinion of the trial judge, who had held that the tax exemption awarded to Cooper Union in its 1859 charter had not been repealed by provisions of the General Tax Law passed by the legislature in 1896. The Court of Appeals noted in a later case that the terms of the exemption provided in the special act of incorporation of Cooper Union had been accepted and relied on by Peter Cooper, thereby constituting a contract protected under the U.S. Constitution.

The tax-exempt income from the Vanderbilt Flats property proved to be very valuable to Cooper Union for a number of years, but it became substantially more valuable when the Chrysler Building was erected on the site in 1930. Most of Cooper Union's Chrysler Building income has since come from what are called tax-equivalency payments, equal to what would normally be paid in property taxes. According to a recent Cooper Union report, the Chrysler Building land currently generates approximately $9 million in annual rent payments and $18 million in annual tax equivalency payments to Cooper Union. Despite projections of greater future income from rent and tax equivalency payments, beginning in 2018, Cooper Union began

charging tuition in 2014, leading to protests, a lawsuit and a settlement that is aimed at improved governance and a possible path back
to free tuition.

Honoring Parsons after his death in 1915, his fellow trustees
(Andrew Carnegie, R. Fulton Cutting, Peter Cooper Hewitt, and J.
P. Morgan) passed a resolution that said in part: "This institution is
particularly indebted to him and his law partners for the success with
which they defended the provision of the Union's Charter granting
it immunity from taxation when the city's authorities attempted to
impose taxation upon it." They could not imagine how much Cooper
Union would benefit in the years to come from Parsons's preserving
the tax exemption he had so firmly established at its incorporation in
1859.

Parsons's extraordinary record of service over fifty-six years was
further recognized at Cooper Union's Founder's Day in 1915. On
that occasion, President Cutting identified what made Parsons so
effective as a leader and advisor: "Skillful in negotiation, sound in
judgment, patient but decisive in action, his unusual business capacity
was employed to the great advantage of the Union . . ."

Chapter Six

More than a Lawyer

Parsons's success as a lawyer and in his many public roles was due in large measure to the loving support he received from his wife Mary during their forty years of marriage. She was a daughter of Catherine Dumesnil, a native of Kentucky, whose father, Antoine Dumesnil, had a colorful background. Sent from France by his family to French Mauritius to escape the revolution in France, Antoine was captured by pirates, escaped, and landed eventually in Boston where he worked as a jewelry manufacturer and merchant. When a ship he had invested in sank, he was forced to sell his business and take his family south to Kentucky.

Catherine Dumesnil married Bowes Reed McIlvaine, a successful merchant and insurance executive whose ancestors included a senator and governor of New Jersey as well as a governor of Pennsylvania. The newlywed couple relocated to New York City shortly after their marriage. Commenting on the marriage, a Louisville newspaper described Catherine as "a young lady of great amiability and beauty."

Mary's southern and French heritage contrasted well with Parsons's Yankee and Dutch colonial roots. During their courtship, they discovered their mutual love of classical music, especially opera, which

Parsons as a young man (courtesy of Lenox Library Association)

continued throughout their married life. Often they attended concerts with friends, including the noted diarist and socialite George Templeton Strong. In October of 1855, Strong wrote of dining at the Fulton market on oysters and going "thereafter to the Philharmonic rehearsal with a group that included little [Mary] McIlvaine."

Strong was clearly an admirer of the much younger Mary, writing in his diary about a group of friends at a gathering in December 1854, among whom were "Miss 'Tote' Anthon and Miss Mary McIlvaine [who] were as good and honest as usual. I prefer them to the most exquisitely elaborated damsels of 'society.' They *seem*, at least, to be more . . . single-hearted . . ."

In November 1855, only a few months before Parsons proposed to Mary (after a concert), Strong still thought enough of her to write in his diary: "Am smoking the pipe of meditation over the fragrant memory of the Philharmonic concert just ended. Miss Mary McIlvaine dined here and went with us . . ."

Parsons had just turned twenty-seven and Mary was twenty-two when they were married in New York on November 5, 1856. The ceremony was performed by her uncle, Charles P. McIlvaine, the Episcopal Bishop of Ohio. Even though his grandfather, Ebenezer Clark, might have preferred that Parsons was marrying a Presbyterian, he should have been somewhat consoled to know that Bishop McIlvaine was known as the leading "low" Episcopalian churchman of his day.

The young couple moved into a brownstone residence in the newly fashionable area near Madison Square Park. Edith Wharton's parents lived a block north, and Theodore Roosevelt was born in 1858 at his parent's home just a few blocks east. On the west side of the park, the luxurious Fifth Avenue Hotel was erected in 1859 by developer Amos Eno (a friend and client of Parsons), which featured the city's first elevators, among its many modern amenities.

Less than a year after their marriage, the Parsons, along with many other New Yorkers, were in the throes of the "Panic of 1857." Fortunately, the income earned by Parsons from his law practice plus the financial resources Mary brought to the marriage made it possible for them to afford a comfortable home in an attractive neighborhood. At this stage of their marriage, however, it was not on the scale described by Isabella Bird in her 1854 book, *The Englishwoman in America*:

> The magnificence of the private dwellings of New York must not escape attention . . . The squares, and many of the numbered streets, contain very superb houses of a very pleasing uniformity of style . . . These houses are six stories high, and usually contain three reception rooms; a dining room, small and not striking in appearance in any way, as dinner parties are seldom given in New York; a small, elegantly furnished drawing-room, used as a family sitting room, and for the reception of morning visitors; and a magnificent reception-room, furnished in the height of taste and elegance, for dancing, music, and evening parties.

In September of 1857, Mary gave birth to a son, named for his grandfather, Edward Lamb Parsons, who had died in the shipwreck almost twenty years earlier. It was a blessing that Matilda Parsons, who died in 1858, lived long enough to enjoy the arrival of her first Parsons grandchild (her daughter, Anna Corning, had given birth to twin sons in Rye in July 1857).

Life in New York City in the 1850s could be challenging even for families like the Parsons, who lived in the better neighborhoods. William Chambers, an Edinburgh publisher, wrote of his visit to the city in 1853 that, "The necessity for seeking vehicular conveyance arises not more from the extreme length of the city than the condition of the principal thoroughfares. I am indeed sorry to hint that New York is . . . not so clean as it might be . . . The mire was ankle-deep in Broadway, and the more narrow streets were barely passable."

According to Frederick Van Wyck, in his *Recollections of an Old New Yorker*, it was not until 1847 that the first houses in New York were connected with the sewers, and even as late as 1863, most houses had outhouses in their back yards. The more substantial houses had bathrooms with tin tubs enclosed in wood, and a tin shower similar to the spray on a watering can. The street watering carts were large barrels on wheels, drawn by horses, and the watering was paid for by those residents who used the service so, as Van Wyck recalled, "the city was patches of wets and drys."

Much of the crime and vice occurred in the area known as Five Points in lower Manhattan, not far from Parsons's law office at 49 Wall Street but still at some distance from their home on West Twenty-Second Street. However, in the summer of 1857 a fight that began downtown between two gangs, the Dead Rabbits and the Bowery Boys, escalated into a citywide gang war. During the two days of mayhem, George Templeton Strong wrote in his diary: "We are in a state of siege, and if half the stories are true, in something like a state of anarchy. There are rumors of . . . houses sacked in the Fifth Avenue near Twenty-Eighth Street . . ."

By 1859, when Mary gave birth to a daughter named Catherine, the increasingly efficient train service between New York City and Rye made it even easier to escape into the healthy countryside. There were a number of Parsons family members to visit there, including John's brother William, who had acquired the home of their Clark grandparents. Although Lounsberry had been sold by Matilda in 1850, it returned to the family when it was purchased in 1858 by John's paternal uncle, James Hewitt Parsons. James and his family continued to use Lounsberry as their country home until 1893, when Parsons purchased it from his widowed aunt.

All was going well for John and Mary in the early years of their marriage, but the year 1861 proved disastrous for them. In June, their two children, who were two and four, died within days of each other from what was described in a joint death notice only as "a short and severe illness." This family tragedy happened in the midst of the great upheaval in New York and all around the country following the outbreak of the Civil War.

After the capture of Fort Sumter by Confederate troops on April 13, 1861, President Lincoln issued a proclamation summoning 75,000 members of the National Guard to Washington in defense of the nation's capital. New York City and its port had no protection other than the police, or as the *Times* put it: "New York was left almost without a corporal's guard."

The mood of many at that time was reflected in a diary entry by George Templeton Strong on April 23, 1861: "Everyone's future has changed in these six months past. This is to be a terrible, ruinous war, and a war in which the nation cannot succeed . . . I was prosperous and well off last November. I believe my assets to be reduced fifty per cent, at least . . . I clearly see this is a most severe personal calamity to me, but I welcome it cordially, for it has shown that I belong to a community that is brave and generous, and that the City of New York is not sordid and selfish."

On April 20, the largest public meeting ever seen in the country, called the Great Sumter Rally, was held at Union Square. Following the rally a Union Defense Committee was formed by the heads of commercial and financial firms, as well as lawyers and other professional men. Its purpose was to organize, arm and equip a home guard to protect the city, funded largely with private donations. At a meeting on May 13, 1861, a brigade named the "Union Grays" was organized, which was soon absorbed into the Twenty-second New York Volunteer Regiment.

Parsons was among the first to join the unit and, although he lacked prior military experience, he was selected as captain of one of the companies because of his organizational and leadership abilities. Two of his good friends and fellow lawyers, George de Forest Lord, and Benjamin F. Butler, were also among the original officers in the Union Grays, which was led by Lieutenant-Colonel (later Brigadier General) Lloyd Aspinwall, a prominent New York shipping executive.

Within a short period of time Parsons managed to engage a drill master, find space and schedule the drills for the men of his company, which were initially set for Mondays and Thursdays from 6 to 10 p.m. over the Opera livery stables on Thirty-second Street and Fourth Avenue. On May 24, he sent a report to headquarters stating that he had under his command in Company H a roster comprised of one first lieutenant, one second lieutenant, five sergeants, four corporals and a total of forty-eight rank and file, including the non-commissioned officers.

He also reported that his men had been using the required drill manual known as "Hardee's Tactics," written by a West Point graduate who was then a colonel in the Confederate Army. Acknowledging that "the company had advanced somewhat irregularly, having failed until now to obtain constant and systematic drill instruction," Parsons assured Aspinwall that, "we are earnest to advance." He also noted that uniforms and rifles were in short supply as they were waiting for a shipment of Enfield rifles to arrive from England and were ordering gray uniforms at a cost of $25 each plus $9 for an overcoat.

A consortium of banks and insurance companies had agreed to underwrite the entire cost of the rifles and uniforms. In the meantime, however, the Union Grays and other units of the home guard were largely self-supporting. Almost everything was paid for by the men, even including the rent of the armories, causing one member of the company to tender his resignation to Parsons because of the expense.

The tragic deaths of both children took a heavy toll on Parsons and his wife. In order to help them get through their bereavement Parsons quickly arranged a trip that would take him and his wife to Europe. First, however, he tendered his resignation as a company commander in the Union Grays. Business transactions and the court calendars, which normally slowed in the summer, were greatly disrupted by the growing hostilities, making it possible for him to take time off from his law practice.

According to a regimental history by General George Wingate, commander of the Twenty-second Regiment, the organizers of the Union Grays intended that its mission should be limited to the emergency defense of New York City. At the outset of the war, many people thought that the conflict would be brief, and volunteers frequently signed up for only ninety days. During the summer of 1861, however, the regiment's officers voted almost unanimously to be mustered into state service as part of the regular National Guard in order to be available for action wherever they might be needed. Unknown to Parsons, his letter of resignation was refused by members of his company, who hoped he would change his mind.

The Parsons left New York in early July on the *S.S. Arago*, a wooden paddle steamer owned by the New York and Havre Steam Navigation Company. Its destination was Le Havre, France, with a stop at Southampton, England, where the Parsons got off. They carried with them letters of introduction to a number of individuals in London, Cambridge and elsewhere in England and on the continent. On their way to Scotland, they visited the village of Cubbington in Warwickshire, the ancestral home of the Parsons family, as well as Manchester, where Parsons's father was buried.

In the two months they were away, their travels took them to Paris, Rome and Florence. Just before returning in September they went to Geneva, where Parsons attended an Evangelical Christian Conference. Their return voyage was on the *S.S. Fulton*, sister ship to the *Arago*. Both ships continued to carry transatlantic passengers and mail until the end of 1861 when they were chartered by the U.S. War Department as transport vessels.

When Parsons returned from Europe, he discovered that his resignation had not been accepted. He was, therefore, still officially a captain and company commander when the Twenty-second Volunteer Regiment was sworn in as part of the Fourth Brigade of the New York National Guard before General Ambrose Burnside. The *Times* reported that it was "an entirely new regiment, having been formed in the past few months, and numbers among its members—both officers and privates—many young men of our most respectable and well-known families." Although he was not present at the ceremony, Parsons and his fellow officers received their regular commissions on October 4, and a formal presentation of colors was made to the regiment on October 16.

On November 27, 1861, he wrote a letter to "My friends of Company H, Union Grays, 22nd Regt: When in June last, under the pressure of a bereavement known to most of you, and in consequence of an absence made necessary by it, I tendered my resignation as your commanding officer, I hoped that you would immediately accept it and fill my place with one more competent to perform its duties . . . I learned on my return that you had pursued a different course . . . due to the loss of which I have alluded, I find, after delaying for sufficient time to verify my fear, no choice, and I should be constrained to renew my resignation did I not also feel that the company at this juncture needs for its head one more competent than within any reasonable time I could hope to become . . . I withdraw from its command with sincere regret at severing a connection which promised so pleasantly . . ."

Parsons's resignation from the National Guard, which took effect in January of 1862, meant that he would not risk being separated from his wife, who was then pregnant. The birth in February of their third child, a son named Reed McIlvaine, helped them recover from their lingering grief. However, the boy lived only five years. Of the eleven children that Mary bore, only five lived beyond age twenty-five.

When orders were finally issued for the Twenty-second Regiment to leave for Washington, the regiment assembled on May 28 and marched to Lafayette Place. As recalled by General Wingate, "As the hour of departure arrived, the regiment formed in columns of companies, surrounded by a throng of enthusiastic friends and relatives . . . Throughout the entire length of Broadway, colored fires burned as the regiment approached, and in passing the Astor House, the sky was illuminated with a discharge of fireworks."

Although Parsons was no longer a member of the regiment when it departed for the front, he was an honored participant in the fiftieth-anniversary celebration of the occasion in 1912. General Wingate sent him a personal letter of invitation, saying: "I earnestly hope that you may be able to join in the parade and attend the dinner, and the committee will consider it a favor to call upon you to say a few words in regard to your recollection of the conditions in 1861 that led to the formation of the regiment."

As the Civil War dragged on, New York City benefitted as the center of increasing commercial and financial activity. In March of 1863, William E. Dodge, a friend and law client of Parsons, wrote a colleague in England: "Things here in the North are in a great state of prosperity . . . The large amount expended by the government has given activity to everything and but for the daily news from the War in the papers and the crowds of soldiers you see about you in the streets you would have no idea of any war. Our streets are crowded, hotels full, the railroads and manufacturers of all kinds except cotton were never doing so well and business generally is active."

The prolonged war nonetheless took a toll on New York's poor as prices rose faster than incomes while the government often delayed sending wages to families of soldiers on active duty. The period of prosperity was shattered in New York when bloody assaults on blacks were committed in July of 1863 by armed mobs during four days of draft riots.

Angered by the new federal conscription law, the rioters burned the Colored Orphan Asylum and ransacked the Colored Sailor's Home. The *Times* estimated that, in addition to numerous fatalities (including at least ten lynchings), 3,000 black residents (out of a black population of 12,000, and total city population of 800,000) were left homeless in the aftermath of the riots.

Joseph Choate, a close friend and neighbor of Parsons, wrote his mother in Massachusetts: "In our immediate neighborhood in 21st Street, there has been no outbreak, but in addition to our two servants, we had four helpless negroes under our roof for shelter—they were being murdered in all parts of the city and no negro out of doors was safe."

Seeking a way to help improve the lives of poor and working class children, Parsons headed a group of young men who started a mission Sunday school in 1857 for the children living in tenements on the lower east side. He acted for twenty years as superintendent of the school, which eventually become a mission of the Brick Presbyterian Church. The success of the mission chapel, which opened in 1867, was shown by the attendance at the first Christmas service of nine hundred children and six hundred adults.

In 1909, a history of the Brick Presbyterian Church included a testimonial to Parsons for the countless hours he had devoted to the mission of the Sunday school, "which was enjoying great prosperity. For this it was indebted, under God, to the unselfish devotion of the workers and, especially, to John E. Parsons, who, during all these years and until 1877, was its head . . . By the inspiration derived from his own energetic leadership, these teachers formed and maintained one of the most extensive and flourishing missions in the city . . . the estimate, which the friends of the mission have formed of Mr. Parsons's work has been heightened by the consideration that it was sustained through the severe and growing pressure of professional duties."

The following year, Parsons received additional praise for this achievement from Ray Stannard Baker. In his 1910 book, *The Spiritual Unrest*, Baker wrote about some of the promising social work being done by a small number of churches in New York City and singled out the work of Parsons, referring to him as "a distinguished lawyer and director of the Sugar Trust." It was an unusual accolade from a noted muck-raking journalist, who had no love for big business and the trusts.

Managing the Brick Church Sunday school was the first of many ways in which Parsons helped to improve the lives of poor and working class children. The most notable of these endeavors were his long service as a trustee of Cooper Union, which provided free higher education to thousands of students and the purchase of a small hotel near his estate in Lenox, Massachusetts, that he used as a summer home for Fresh Air children from the tenements of New York for many years.

He was motivated in part by a desire to honor the memory of his own children who died at a young age during the 1860s. It was a happier time for the Parsons family, however, in June of 1874 when they all traveled to Europe shortly after the birth of the youngest child. A newspaper reported that they sailed on board the steamship, *Queen*, bound for Liverpool with five children: Mary (ten), Edith (nine), Helen (seven), Herbert (five), Gertrude (four) and baby Constance (one) as well as two maids. The trip was all the more remarkable because it occurred in the midst of the economic upheaval known as the "Panic of 1873."

Chapter Seven

The Bar Association
and Boss Tweed

In his 1868 book *Sunshine and Shadow in New York,* Matthew Hale Smith painted a generally unflattering portrait of New York lawyers. Of the more than three thousand lawyers practicing in the city shortly after the Civil War, Smith guessed that "perhaps a hundred are known to each other personally by social relations or otherwise; another hundred by their professional or business intercourse; and the rest are unknown to each other, even by reputation, as if they resided in the antipodes."

A large number of the leading members of the bar gathered on January 14, 1869 in the banqueting room at Delmonico's restaurant in lower Manhattan. According to an account of the event, "Almost every notability in city professional life was there," and they dined on "viands of the most exquisite qualities." The guest of honor on that occasion was James W. Gerard, who was retiring from the practice of law after forty-five years. Parsons, who had learned his basic courtroom skills as a law clerk in Gerard's firm, was on hand to toast his early mentor.

Tammany Hall Boss Tweed, by Thomas Nast (permission of Everett Historical /Shutterstock)

Just a few months earlier, Parsons had joined many of the same lawyers at a similar banquet at the Astor House hotel in honor of William M. Evarts, another distinguished New York lawyer, who had recently become the attorney general in President Andrew Johnson's administration. On both these occasions, the toasts, as reported in the press, were full of praise for the honorees, the legal profession and the judiciary.

Despite the atmosphere of optimism and camaraderie enjoyed by the elite lawyers and judges on those two occasions, the New York Bar and judiciary were facing a crisis. A number of scandals had linked some prominent lawyers to Tammany Hall politicians and to robber barons like Cornelius Vanderbilt and Jay Gould. Well publicized court battles over control of the Erie Railroad implicated some leading lawyers and judges in unethical legal tactics and dubious judicial behavior.

In June 1869, an editorial in the *Times* stated that, "All lawyers in active practice are aware of instances in which judges on the bench influence or intimidate members of the Bar." It went on to propose as a remedy "a permanent, strong and influential association of lawyers for mutual protection and benefit," adding that, "in London and Liverpool such associations have been found necessary and effective . . . Such an organization is sadly needed in this city, and if the respectable members consult their professional interests and expectations, they will form one at an early date."

An even stronger call to arms was issued by the diarist and lawyer, George Templeton Strong, who wrote in December 1869: "The stink of our state judiciary is growing too strongly ammoniac and hippuric for endurance . . . the average New York judge . . . is as bad as the New York alderman, if not worse, because his office is more sacred . . . The nuisance must be abated somehow, and that soon, but I see no hope of its abatement, except by a perilous process, justified only by the extremest necessity, and after all constitutional remedies are exhausted . . . No city can long continue rich and prosperous that tolerates abuses like these. Capital will flee to safer quarters."

That same month, Parsons joined with other prominent New York lawyers who shared Strong's concerns and pledged to unite in forming an association to "promote the interests of the public" and "sustain the profession in its proper position in the community." By February 15, 1870, a constitution, drafted by Parsons and others, was adopted, and more than 200 lawyers had become the original members of the New York City Bar Association (officially known as the Association of the Bar of the City of New York).

The first president of the association was William M. Evarts, who had returned to private practice in New York when Andrew Johnson failed in his bid for reelection. Albon P. Man, Parsons's senior partner, was the association's first treasurer, and Parsons, at the age of forty-one, was selected as one of the youngest members of the executive committee.

To promote expanded membership in the association and support for its mission, the executive committee published a pamphlet that outlined the judicial practices in need of reform:

> Since 1846, the era of our present State Constitution, the barriers to admission to the Bar have been substantially removed; the distinctions between attorney, solicitor and counsellor have been obliterated; the judges have been made elective by the popular vote for a short term only; and a system thus

introduced which has exposed them to partisan influences.

During the same period has come into operation a new system of procedure, which gives the judges so elected larger discretionary powers than ever before and a patronage in the appointment of receivers and referees, and in the granting of fees and allowances, the exercise of which is at least dangerous.

Many of these abuses were perpetrated by the judicial cronies of William M. ("Boss") Tweed, who had seized control of the New York City government in 1869. Operating from his position as a state senator, he and his associates (known as the "Tweed Ring"), controlled the mayor's office, Board of Audit and Public Works.

The downfall of the Tweed Ring began when disgruntled Tammany Hall members leaked incriminating evidence to the *Times* about enormous frauds perpetrated by the officials upon the New York City treasury. Following a series of damning *Times* articles in July 1871, *Harper's Weekly* and other newspapers also exposed the scandal.

While Parsons worked within the bar association on judicial reform, an organization known as the Committee of Seventy carried out plans to attack the fraud and corruption of Tweed and his Ring on a broad front. Collaboration between the two groups resulted in the defeat of a Tweed judicial nominee in the municipal elections of 1871, one of many losses suffered by Tammany candidates that fall.

Emboldened by its election victory, the bar association prepared a detailed report of corruption committed by three state court judges: George Barnard, Albert Cardozo and John McCunn. The report was delivered in early 1872 to the judiciary committee of the State Assembly, which held hearings from February into April of 1872 at a hotel in New York City. The bar association, which was invited to take a leading role in the proceedings, selected Parsons and two other members to handle the prosecution.

After reviewing the extensive record of the hearings, during which Parsons and his co-counsel examined more than two hundred witnesses, the committee recommended impeachment of the three judges. The case against Cardozo, who was generally considered the worst of the lot, was dropped when he decided to resign from the bench. Once the Assembly voted to impeach Barnard and McCunn, the Senate held separate impeachment trials of the two judges.

The trial against Judge John McCunn was held in the Senate Chamber at Albany with Parsons, Van Cott and Albert Stickney again acting as lead counsel on behalf of the state. Just prior to the trial, an editorial in the *Times* indicated some concern about the outcome: "Judge McCunn may be acquitted, but there will be no partisan whitewash thick enough to hide the filthiness of the hands that burlesqued justice by putting him in the seat of justice . . ."

McCunn was notorious for naturalizing large numbers of immigrants just prior to elections. According to various accounts, he mass-produced more than 17,000 citizens in one month while Barnard was naturalizing another 10,000 new voters. All this fraudulent activity caused the *Tribune* to quip that "Judge McCunn has naturalized all the lower counties of Ireland, beginning at Tipperary and running down to Cork. Judge Barnard will arrange for the northern counties at the next sitting of chambers."

To avoid challenging the citizenship of thousands of New Yorkers, however, Parsons and his co-counsel were careful that the eight charges against McCunn made no reference to any of his illegal naturalizations. The trial ran from June 18 to July 2 when, following a long and detailed summation of the case by Parsons, McCunn was found guilty and removed from office. Less than a week later he died from natural causes, but his obituary in the *Times* was merciless: "In person, he was popular with the rougher classes . . . As a politician, he was mistrusted even by those with whom he labored."

With only a short break, Parsons and his fellow prosecutors began the impeachment trial of Judge George Barnard, which lasted five weeks and resulted in a verdict of guilty on twenty-six of the thirty-nine articles in the indictment. When Barnard died in 1879, the *Times* carried a more charitable obituary than the one for McCunn. It recalled that despite his Tammany connections, Barnard had issued an injunction on the New York City controller, restraining him from spending more of the city's money, which it noted "aided materially in the overthrow of the 'Tweed Ring.'"

During the course of six months, Parsons, Van Cott and Stickney had devoted most of their time and legal expertise to prosecuting the corrupt judges with very little compensation for their efforts from either the bar association or the state. Although the three lawyers may have been able to spend some time on their private practices while the hearings were in New York City, they were required to be in Albany for the McCunn trial and in Saratoga for Barnard's proceedings.

Tweed would have been tried earlier but for a dispute over court jurisdiction engineered by a talented team of lawyers, headed by David Dudley Field. The first criminal trial, held in January 1873, resulted in a hung jury, allowing Tweed to retain his seat in the state Senate. In March, the New York State Senate began hearings into Tweed's corrupt activities while serving as a senator, and retained Parsons to interrogate him.

First, Tweed claimed he had never taken the oath of office and, further, that his persistent failure to perform his duties meant the seat was virtually vacant. The wily politician then managed to avoid being expelled or impeached by resigning his seat. Tweed's political career finally came to an end in November 1873 when he was retried and found guilty on fifty-one of the fifty-five offenses charged.

Tweed received a sentence of twelve years in prison and a $12,750 fine, but the Court of Appeals reduced the sentence to $250 and time served. The day after his release, Tweed was arrested again on civil charges and returned to jail where he enjoyed special privileges, including supervised visits to his home. It was during a family visit in December 1875 that Tweed escaped his jailer and fled. He escaped to Cuba and then to Spain, where he was identified and returned to a New York jail, where he died in April of 1878.

More fortunate than Tweed was Abraham Oakey Hall, who was accused of acting as front man for the Tweed Ring while he was mayor from 1868 to 1872. Hall was indicted and tried three times but was acquitted in each case. A graduate of NYU in the class of 1844 (four years ahead of Parsons), he served on the NYU council with Parsons for a number of years.

Parsons was also retained in 1872 as special counsel by Mayor Hall to prosecute another member of the Tweed Ring, Henry W. Genet, for fraud. Genet, a New York State Senator and Tweed adviser, was convicted of billing for iron work intended for the Harlem Court House that was never delivered. Like Tweed himself, Genet escaped from custody and fled to Europe. Some years later he returned, was sent to prison and, upon his release, ran unsuccessfully for alderman.

His successes with the Tweed Ring led to the appointment of

Parsons by the New York attorney general to investigate and bring
suits against a number of Brooklyn contractors and officials during the
mid-1870s. His courtroom appearances were also receiving increased
newspaper coverage. Interviewing Parsons about a delay in the trials
of the so-called "Brooklyn Ring," a reporter from the *Brooklyn Eagle*
described him as "a gentleman, forty-five years of age, who in his
appearance combines the evident ability of a lawyer with the cultured
manners of the old school. He is rather above medium height, well-
built, with aquiline features, bright blue eyes and side whiskers."

When the reporter asked whether the trial delay was due to concerns about compensation for his work, Parsons replied that, "After I
assumed the prosecutions, I was committed to see them through even
though they will not cover all expenses. Whether or not, my clients
are the People of the State of New York, although the Legislature
is not very liberal in compensating counsel . . . Although I made a
considerable sacrifice for the Barnard trial, I am far from regretting it,
and should the present proceedings have no different result, I should
be equally content."

In the memorial to Parsons in the bar association's 1915 yearbook, Joseph Choate wrote, "By the able part that he took in the
[impeachment] proceedings he rendered an inestimable service to the
People of New York and to the cause of justice everywhere that ought
never to be forgotten . . . It required a great deal of courage, a vastly
greater amount of persistent and unremitting toil, and a legal ability
of the highest order to bring about this notable historical result, and
Mr. Parsons and his associates received the award of appreciation and
applause which they so justly deserved."

Chapter Eight
Swallowtail Reformer

Testifying at a Congressional hearing in 1911, Parsons told a House committee investigating the Sugar Trust: "I have never been a party man; I am out of party politics." However, he said at the start of an interview with a *Times* reporter the prior year: "I am an old-time Democrat and was brought up in Westchester County, where it was almost a crime to be anything other than a member of the Democratic Party. Later, when I came to the bar, I was brought into contact with Samuel J. Tilden, who became a friend, and, down to his death, Abram S. Hewitt was my warm personal and professional friend."

It was a curious way for Parsons to frame his answer to a question about his views on Democratic gains in the 1910 mid-term elections. However, it provided some interesting insights into his political philosophy. As an "old-time Democrat," his views were grounded on some fundamental Jacksonian principles. He said in the interview that he hoped "the important members of the party will use their opportunities on the lines I have always associated with the party, namely, economy of administration and recognition of the rights of the State

Greater New York (courtesy of New York Public Library)

as against attempted usurpation by the Federal Government."

As to the problems with the country's political system, Parsons's view was that, "The remedy is in the sound common sense of the people when it is allowed to assert itself. I do not quite believe that *vox populi* [voice of the people] is *vox dei* [voice of God] . . . But after all, our hope must be in those intelligent and capable persons who are best able to give suitable direction to public affairs."

Growing up in the Jacksonian era, his political views were influenced by his youthful experience in Rye, a small community in New York's Westchester County. Although close to New York City, Westchester was a very rural area before the railroads arrived in the mid-nineteenth century. It was populated largely by small farmers, tradesmen, millers and artisans, a majority of whom voted consistently for Democratic candidates in presidential elections from 1828 (Jackson) through 1892 (Cleveland).

The person who influenced him most in his youth was his grandfather, Ebenezer Clark, a wealthy merchant who had moved his family from New York City for a healthier and more communal life in the village of Rye. For Parsons, his grandfather was a prime example of "those intelligent and capable persons who are best able to give suitable direction to public affairs."

It was in that context that Parsons referred to his friends, Samuel J. Tilden and Abram S. Hewitt (who managed Tilden's unsuccessful campaign for President in 1876). They became prominent leaders of the reform movement that restored the credibility of the Democratic Party in New York by reorganizing Tammany Hall after the collapse of the Tweed Ring in the early 1870s.

Some of these reformers (called "Swallowtails" because of their

penchant for wearing tail coats) became actively engaged in party politics or provided the necessary finances. Parsons and other leaders of
the bar association concentrated on reforming the judiciary, joining
forces with Tilden, then a member of the New York State Assembly,
to overcome political obstacles in Albany and win impeachment of
the corrupt judges.

In his classic study, *Power and Society: Greater New York at
the Turn of the Century*, David C. Hammack describes the evolution of New York City's politics in the latter part of the nineteenth
century:

> In reality, the city's politics reflected the increasing com-
> plexity of its economic and social life, with the years between
> 1886 and 1903 serving as a Transition Period between the
> merchant-dominated polity of an earlier era and the Tamma-
> ny-managed city of the first-third of the twentieth century.
> In the earlier years, merchants dominated municipal politics,
> just as they dominated the municipal economy, and after
> the 1870 ouster of the Tweed Ring they dominated quite
> openly. During what can be called the Era of the Swallowtails,
> 1872–1886, every man elected Mayor of New York City was
> a prominent merchant who owed his nomination to the most
> politically active group of Democrats among the merchants,
> bankers and lawyers who directed the city's economy.

One of those merchant mayors was Parsons's friend and law client, Edward Cooper, who was the son of Peter Cooper and brother-
in-law of Abram S. Hewitt. Cooper was elected mayor in 1878 as

a fusion candidate with support from Republican and independent voters. Cooper spent much of his two-year term trying to reform the corrupt police department, but he did manage to spearhead legislative reforms to improve the city's terrible tenement conditions.

In the election of 1886, Hewitt, who was then Tammany's compromise candidate for mayor, defeated the United Labor candidate, Henry George, and the Republican, Theodore Roosevelt, who was just getting started in politics. The race, one of the most interesting in the city's history, was hotly contested. Ironically, Hewitt, one of the wealthiest New Yorkers, accused Roosevelt of being a tool of rich businessmen and ended up gaining the votes of a substantial number of Republicans who were afraid of George's radical programs.

Commenting on Hewitt's one term as mayor, historian Richard Brookhiser wrote that he "was an old-fashioned Jackson Democrat, in favor of low tariffs and hard money [but] he had a troubled term. He alienated Tammany Hall . . . for he cracked down on gambling, whoring and saloons that broke the blue laws . . . Clearly, his cunning had deserted him. When he stood for reelection two years later [Tammany's leaders] combined to unseat him."

During the years that Hewitt and Cooper were actively involved in politics, they continued their close collaboration with Parsons on the board of Cooper Union and relied on him as legal adviser for themselves, the Cooper family and their business interests. Both of them remained in senior management positions at several companies, including a glue factory, which was one of the sources of Peter Cooper's fortune.

In 1885, Parsons won a case for the Peter Cooper Glue Factory, in which the court ruled that the company owed taxes to New York

City but not Brooklyn, which was then a separate city, even though it had offices in both locations. It was a particularly good result not only because it avoided double taxation, but also because Hewitt did not have to worry about charges of tax evasion at the start of his campaign to become mayor of New York City.

Although Parsons avoided active participation in party politics, he told a large group assembled at his eighty-fifth birthday celebration in 1914 that "in looking back at my own experience I have often felt as if . . . I should not have so studiously, so carefully and so continuously abstained from anything like public life."

However, he worked constantly for social and political reforms, initially as a prominent Presbyterian layman. For forty years he served as a board member and *pro bono* legal counsel of the United Presbyterian Church's Board of Home Missions. His involvement in mission work began with the Sunday school that he started in 1857 and later moved to the Brick Presbyterian Church, where he served as a Ruling Elder, long-time trustee and board president.

Through his Presbyterian and ecumenical activities, he worked closely with prominent members of the Protestant clergy. One of the most notable of these men was the Rev. Charles Parkhurst, whom he first met in Lenox, Massachusetts, where Parsons had a summer home. Parkhurst, who became pastor of the Congregational Church in Lenox in 1874 was influenced by Parsons in 1880 to move with his family to New York City and become minister of the Madison Square Presbyterian Church.

For a number of years, Parkhurst built a reputation as a gifted preacher to an affluent congregation. However, he gradually became so alarmed by the rampant criminal activity in the city that he agreed in 1891 to become head of the Society for the Prevention of Crime, which had been founded in 1877. In February of 1892, Parkhurst preached a sermon condemning Tammany Hall and the police for their roles in the graft, prostitution and other unlawful activity throughout the city.

When a grand jury required him to produce hard evidence, Parkhurst personally hired a private detective and went with him and a friend in disguise into the worst neighborhoods to collect proof of the corruption. After visiting numerous brothels and saloons, he told his friend that, "the unspeakable horror of [those places] tells more than I could in a million sermons." He went on to present more than enough evidence of crime and vice in a second sermon to shake up the police department.

Beginning in the 1890s, Parsons became actively involved in the nonpartisan movement to achieve political reform that allied Republicans, Democrats and independents in support of fusion tickets. According to David Hammack, "For about ten years the independents were, as a whole, remarkably effective in winning votes. The result was a series of vigorous fusion campaigns in 1890, 1894, 1901 and 1903; an impressive independent campaign in 1897; and resounding fusion victories in 1894 and 1901."

In 1894, Parsons was a principal speaker at a meeting in support of William Strong for election as a reform mayor. He told the audience, "The question in the coming election is not one of party, but of opposition to Tammany Hall and the enemies of good government." The meeting was organized by the City Club of New York, an organization founded in 1892 that concentrated on promoting bipartisanship in municipal government and reforming the judiciary.

The reform momentum also resulted in creation of a bi-partisan Board of Police Commissioners with Theodore Roosevelt as its president.

At a dinner to honor Parkhurst in 1895, Parsons joined with Roosevelt and in support of the non-partisan ticket in the upcoming elections. Roosevelt strongly endorsed the fusion ticket while stressing that he was still a "strong [Republican] party man." He also called Parkhurst "the mainspring of the mightiest revolution in municipal politics seen on this continent." Parsons also spoke strongly in favor of the fusion ticket and praised his good friend Parkhurst for his dedication to municipal reform.

When Parsons became president of the City Club in 1896 the ranks of reformers had become divided over the proposal to form what was called "Greater New York." It required adopting a new charter that would consolidate the existing city of New York (mainly Manhattan) with its neighboring communities of Brooklyn, the eastern Bronx, most of Queens and Staten Island.

Supporters of consolidation included some reformers who thought it would lead to more efficient government, but opponents argued that it gave the mayor too much power. Parsons, as president of the City Club, strongly opposed the charter. He warned that the enlarged metropolis would lack effective administrative and financial controls, which would allow public officials too many opportunities to waste money and pad payrolls.

In March 1897, his detailed objections to both the form and substance of the proposed charter were reported in the *Times*, ending with his observation that, "Apparently, the scheme is favored by the leaders of both political parties. Each sees potential advantages in the accomplishment of the scheme. I think the present city will be the victim."

Despite the efforts of Parsons and many other reformers, the combined power of the two political parties succeeded in the consolidation of Greater New York. According to the authors of *Gotham: A History of New York City to 1898*: "Though New York good government forces assailed the final product, Brooklynites professed general satisfaction (or exhaustion), and with Tammany boss Croker's support, Republican boss Platt got the nine-hundred-page document through the legislature . . . After one last stubborn veto from Mayor William Strong had been overcome, the Charter of Greater New York was presented to Governor Frank Black for his signature, which was affixed on May 5, 1897."

At the time Parsons became president of the City Club in 1896, the *Times* reported that the membership of the club had "seriously decreased." However, after completion of his term as president, the *Times* noted in 1901 that, "The membership of the City Club is rapidly increasing, and among the latest names proposed is that of John D. Rockefeller."

In 1900, Parsons was elected president of the New York City Bar Association, in recognition of his many contributions since its founding three decades earlier. Its role in government reform had diminished over the years as organizations like the City Club and Citizens Union took the lead, but under Parsons, the association continued to keep a close watch on any signs that Tammany was gaining renewed control of the judiciary.

At an age when most of his contemporaries were reducing their business and professional activities, Parsons remained heavily involved in both his legal practice and his many charitable and civic organizations. His remarkable vitality may have been due in part to the pleasure he derived from working closely with his son in their law practice.

Herbert Parsons received his college education at Yale and, after graduating from Harvard Law School, he entered his father's law firm of Parsons, Shepard & Ogden in 1894. Although his father was an independent Democrat, Herbert had decided at Yale to become a Republican and got actively involved in the Republican County Organization not long after his admission to the bar.

As he rose through the ranks, Herbert became a close friend and political protégé of Theodore Roosevelt. When Herbert died from an accident in 1925, his obituary in the *Times* said: "He was one of the younger men selected by Theodore Roosevelt to carry on the fight against the old-line bosses whom Colonel Roosevelt wanted to put out of business."

When Roosevelt ran for New York State governor in 1898, John Parsons backed him, saying, "I hope that the [Republican] Party will nominate him and the Independents will endorse him, that everyone will vote for him and that he will be elected." With Roosevelt's support, Herbert won elections in 1899 and 1901 as a New York City Alderman on the fusion ticket, thereby making common cause with his father.

In 1904, Herbert won the first of three terms as a congressman from New York City's "silk stocking" district, helped by Roosevelt's landslide victory in the presidential election. However, the senior Parsons actively supported Roosevelt's Democratic opponent, Judge Alton B. Parker who had resigned as chief judge of the New York Court of Appeals to accept the nomination.

As one of the leaders of a large group of New York lawyers calling themselves the "Constitution Club," Parsons signed a declaration of principles that emphasized the separation of powers under the Constitution and stated, "This venerable and beneficent policy President Roosevelt has undertaken to reverse, and in its place to substitute a policy of autocratic force. He has shown that a president who has the will to usurp legislative functions, to exalt the power of the Executive above the Constitution and to commit our nation to violations of international law, easily finds a way."

Parsons must have carefully considered whether his strong criticism of Roosevelt would be damaging to Herbert's own campaign and, rightly, concluded that it would not. It is not clear why Parsons, at the age of seventy-five, decided to become so publicly partisan. Yet, it may be that he saw Roosevelt's campaign to "bust" the trusts, including the Sugar Trust, as a prime example of how he was usurping legislative functions and exalting the Executive over the Constitution.

Chapter Nine
Plutocrats and Philanthropists

I n 1883, Parsons lost two of his closest friends and mentors with the deaths of Peter Cooper and William E. Dodge. They were among the pioneers of what Charles and Mary Beard called "the spreading plutocracy" of the post–Civil War era. They were also role models for the new generation of New York's civic leaders and philanthropists that was emerging at the dawn of the Gilded Age.

The funeral services for Dodge, according to the *Times*, "drew together an assemblage such is seldom seen upon such an occasion . . . There were hundreds of people distinguished in the business and social world, and hundreds of others who had come to pay their modest tribute to the memory of one who had been to them a kind employer or generous benefactor."

The *Times* reported that Dodge's will, "which was in the custody of John E. Parsons," disposed of an estate that was estimated to net about $5 million (worth more than $100 million currently). Among its most valuable assets was a large shareholding of Phelps Dodge, a major mining company he had co-founded. The article highlighted "large bequests to charitable and religious institutions," including several Presbyterian mission societies, the Metropolitan Museum of Art

St. Helen's Home and Fresh Air children (courtesy of the *Berkshire Eagle*)

and the "Museum of Natural History in Central Park."

As historian Maury Klein has observed, "While old money lost its taste and energy for business, it became the driving force behind philanthropy and civic enterprise in New York. Old-money representatives graced the boards of every major cultural institution in service to a notion of stewardship that replaced their vanished economic dominance. Some believed the wealthy had a social responsibility to use their fortunes wisely; others simply wished to provide the city with the trappings of 'culture' in the form of libraries, schools, universities, museums, art galleries, orchestras, operas, and theaters."

In a chapter about the Gilded Age in their classic 1927 work, *The Rise of American Civilization*, the Beards speculated that there were only three millionaires in 1861 but nearly four thousand by the turn of the century. The latter number was most likely based on a national survey published in 1892 by the *New York Tribune*. It not only calculated that there were 4,047 millionaires in the United States, but included the names and sources of wealth of each person, listed by place of residence.

The survey showed that more than one-third of the millionaires lived in New York City, including those in Brooklyn, which in 1892 was still a separate city. Although Peter Cooper and William Dodge were no longer alive, their children all appeared in the survey, along with other clients of Parsons, including Astors (both the William and the John Jacob branches), Havemeyers and Lorillards. Typical entries for some of his clients read:

Henry O. Havemeyer: "Partly inherited; made in the manufacture of sugar and investment of accumulations . . ."

Abram S. Hewitt: "Made in the manufacture of iron, isinglass and glue . . ."

Collis P. Huntington: "A man of very great fortune, amassed chiefly in building and managing the Central Pacific and Southern Pacific Railroads . . ."

Morris K. Jesup: "Importation of iron, banking and investments . . ."

Also included in the list was William H. Parsons (younger brother of John Parsons), whose fortune was derived from the business of paper manufacturing in Maine. Although John Parsons had not achieved millionaire status by 1892, he was listed among the New York millionaires in the 1902 edition of the *World Almanac and Encyclopedia*. The source of his wealth was reported as real estate, but the primary source was the legal fees he earned, especially as general counsel to the Sugar Trust.

Parsons's wealthy clients often sought his advice in making lifetime and testamentary gifts to the recently opened Metropolitan Museum of Art, the Museum of Natural History and other new bastions of New York's cultural life along with the more traditional support for religious and educational institutions. They relied on Parsons's advice not only because of his legal expertise but also because of his broad experience in dealing with nonprofit and charitable organizations. One admiring journalist wrote: "Parsons disproved that old bromide that a good trial lawyer is not a safe counselor."

Yet his reputation as an adviser was more than matched by his skills as a trial lawyer who litigated numerous will contests and estate disputes. One high-profile case involved a multi-millionaire railroad owner named Henry Plant who, shortly before his death, attempted to move his legal residence to Connecticut in order to avoid New York inheritance taxes on his estate, then worth about $18 million. When Plant's widow discovered that the will provided only a lifetime annuity of $30,000 for her, she hired William D. Guthrie, an eminent New York lawyer, to protect her interests and challenge the jurisdiction of the Connecticut courts.

Guthrie, a partner in the law firm of Guthrie, Cravath & Henderson (predecessor to Cravath, Swaine & Moore), advised his client that they should retain Parsons to assist them, saying: "Mr. Parsons is at the head of our bar in will cases and the very strongest associate we could have." Among the opposing counsel was Lewis Cass Ledyard, a partner in Carter, Ledyard and Milburn, a firm that still operates under the same name.

The legal battle was bitterly fought over fourteen years in multiple courts. At one point, Mrs. Plant was examined as an adverse witness by Ledyard. According to Guthrie's account, "Mrs. Plant's testimony was wonderfully effective. She was more than a match for Mr. Ledyard, who treated her in a most brutal and ungentlemanly manner . . . I know of no man who could have borne the strain as well as she did . . . Mr. Parsons said she was a perfect witness."

After the long and acrimonious series of trials and appeals it was finally decided that Plant had never abandoned his New York domicile and, therefore, the Connecticut will was invalid. In 1904, the warring parties agreed to a settlement providing for Mrs. Plant to receive $8.5 million from the estate, which had grown to $23 million. For his valuable services, Parsons was paid a fee of $150,000 while Guthrie is said to have earned $1 million.

Out of her distribution, Mrs. Plant made substantial gifts to charities in memory of her husband, including funds for erection of the Plant Pavilion at St. Luke's Hospital. Guthrie may have helped her plan her charitable giving, but there was no lawyer during the Gilded Age who did more to help the wealthy maintain and distribute their fortunes than Parsons.

A notable example was his role in the famous Fayerweather will contest, which ended in 1904 with a decision by the U.S. Supreme Court after twelve years of legal battles. The decision allowed the executors, represented by Parsons, to carry out the charitable intent of Daniel Fayerweather, a leather merchant, by distributing most of his $6 million estate among numerous colleges and hospitals.

In reporting on the Supreme Court decision, the *Times* noted that "The Fayerweather will contest was one of the hardest fought legal contests in history, and was famous for the notable array of counsel who appeared on one side or the other." Among the thirty-four sets of lawyers involved in the case were Parsons's good friends, Joseph Choate and Elihu Root.

After making specific bequests to charities, the will and codicils, called for the residuary estate to be distributed outright to the executors. However, Fayerweather also signed a memorandum outlining a plan of charitable distribution for the executors to follow. This plan was designed to avoid an 1860 New York statute that required a surviving spouse's consent when more than half of an estate was bequeathed to charities.

Recognizing legal flaws in the estate plan, Parsons advised the executors to sign a deed of gift, which included a cash payment made to the widow in return for her release of her rights under the 1860 statute. The terms of the deed of gift continued to be challenged on various grounds, but the solution crafted by Parsons ultimately achieved the charitable goals of Fayerweather.

At one point in the proceedings, he told the board of the Woman's Hospital, one of the named charitable beneficiaries, that the responsibility for the delay in settling the case "belongs first and last to that profession to which I belong . . . Such a thing as a man giving away a large estate to charity was assumed to imply that he was mentally deranged or under some malign influence."

Parsons raised both of those issues in a case contesting the will of Caroline Merrill, which left the bulk of her estate to Cardinal John McCloskey, the Archbishop of New York. Under a prior will, Mrs. Merrill had named George Merrill, her adopted son and Parsons's client, as her sole beneficiary.

The case was closely followed by the press, which dwelled on testimony about Mrs. Merrill's eccentric behavior and allegations of improper influence on her by members of the clergy. In 1882, after trials and appeals over nearly four years, Parsons succeeded in winning the case for his client by convincing the court that Mrs. Merrill was not sane when she revoked her earlier will. The surrogate said that to rule otherwise would have required him to find that "an intelligent, kind, modest, Christian woman had been turned into an unfeeling, cruel, vulgar and obscene fiend incarnate . . ."

None of Parsons's lawsuits attracted more media attention than the contest over the will of Louis C. Hamersley, who died in 1883 leaving an estate that was valued well above $5 million. The widow, a noted beauty and socialite known as Lily, was granted a life income interest in the residuary estate. The contested will provided that the estate principal at her death would go to male descendants of Louis or, if there were none, then to male descendants of his cousin, J. Hooker Hamersley, who was Parsons's client.

The will was finally admitted to probate in 1886 after lengthy and highly publicized trials involving nearly one hundred contestants, who were represented by more than twenty law firms. One of the highlights of the case was the refusal of a long-time Hamersley family employee, Rebecca Jones, to answer any questions about her employers. As a result, "Silent Becky," as she was nicknamed by the press, was held in contempt and spent more than a year in jail.

Lily Hamersley was once again a news item when she married the Eighth Duke of Marlborough, uncle of Winston Churchill. She became the chatelaine of Blenheim Palace, his family's ancestral home, where her large income was used to purchase a new and much-needed roof for the palace.

After the Duke's death, she next married a British war hero, Lord William Beresford, prompting someone to quip that she married one husband for the money, another for the title and the third for love. At the age of forty-two, Lady Beresford gave birth to a son, who inherited about $7 million from his mother when she died in 1909. However, the remainder of the Hamersley fortune went to his cousin, the son of J. Hooker Hamersley, a client of Parsons.

During the Gilded Age there were several prominent women who were married to Astor men. However, references to "The Mrs. Astor," meant Caroline Webster Schermerhorn Astor, the doyenne of New York society and a client of Parsons. When her husband,

William Backhouse Astor, Jr., died in 1892, his fortune was estimated at upwards of $100 million, most of which was left to his son, John Jacob Astor IV. Caroline Astor received a relatively modest share of the estate, including life interests in their homes in New York City and in Newport, plus a lifetime annuity of $50,000 from a trust.

In 1900, newspapers carried a story that Mrs. Astor's son had petitioned a court to cease payment of the annuity to his mother, based on the language of his father's will, but also, as he claimed, because she had accumulated substantial funds through investments. Representing Mrs. Astor, Parsons was successful in having the court deny the petition.

It was a much different result a century later for the philanthropist and socialite, Brooke Astor, who is said to have inherited roughly $125 million on the death of her husband, Vincent Astor. Late in her life, the news was filled with the prosecution of her son by a previous marriage, Anthony Marshall, who was convicted and sent to jail for stealing funds from his dying mother.

One of the most satisfying estate settlements was the victory Parsons won for Heloise ("Ella") Durant Rose, following another marathon legal battle that was finally decided in 1900. As the *New York World* reported, "It has been a hotly contested case, argued in the drawing rooms of the '400' as much as in the court room." Ella and her brother, William, were the surviving children of Thomas Durant, who died without a will in 1885.

The senior Durant was a promoter of the Union Pacific and principal owner of the Adirondack Railway, but he had lost much of his large fortune in the Credit Mobilier scandal in 1872 during the term of President Grant. William, however, managed to maintain a life of luxury from the remaining estate while paying his sister an allowance of only $100 to $200 a month. Abram Hewitt, one of Ella's friends, retained Parsons, who obtained a judicial order for an estate accounting. After many delays, a court found that Ella was entitled to receive one-third of the remaining estate, worth more than $700,000.

Occasionally, Parsons was on the losing side. One adverse result that was particularly disappointing for Parsons involved the will of a notorious character named Andrew J. Garvey, who had become wealthy through corrupt dealings with "Boss" Tweed. Garvey escaped prosecution by testifying against Tweed and thereafter spent much of his time abroad where he eventually died.

In his will, which was not drawn by Parsons, Garvey left large amounts to various New York charitable institutions, including several hospitals, perhaps to assuage his conscience. One of the hospitals named in the will was the Skin and Cancer Hospital of New York, whose name was similar to the non-related Cancer Hospital.

Parsons, who was president of the Cancer Hospital and represented it as a claimant in the lawsuit, was not allowed by the court to testify about his conversation with Garvey several years before his death about his testamentary plans. The judge ruled that even though his testimony could have proved that the Garvey intended to provide for the Cancer Hospital, the description of the Skin and Cancer Hospital was sufficiently definite for it to be awarded the funds.

Although he was not successful in that case, Parsons managed during his long career to raise extraordinary amounts of money for two of New York's pioneering hospitals, which today operate as parts of The Mount Sinai Medical Center and The Memorial Sloan Kettering Cancer Center.

Chapter Ten
Hospital Pioneer

In the early 1900s, when Parsons was president of the Woman's Hospital, a fundraising brochure referred to its founding by "Doctor J. Marion Sims, whose name stands for all that is most progressive in the modern history of this branch of surgery . . ." Despite that tribute, there was a long history of conflicts between Sims and the Woman's Hospital boards that led to the founding of what is now called the Memorial Sloan Kettering Cancer Center. Much of the credit for the early success of both hospitals belongs to Parsons.

The New York Woman's Hospital, founded in 1855, was the first hospital in America dedicated exclusively to treating female patients. Although Sims has been criticized in recent years for performing experimental surgeries on slave women during his early career in Alabama, he is still widely recognized as the father of American gynecology. He moved to New York in 1853 to increase his clinical experience and expand his reputation after developing the first reliable method for repairing vesicovaginal fistula.

This debilitating condition, suffered as a result of childbirth, had condemned many women to perpetual incontinence. The success of the Sims procedure was hastened by the discovery of ether as an

NEW-YORK CANCER HOSPITAL, CENTRAL PARK WEST AND 106TH STREET.

New-York Cancer Hospital (courtesy of New York Public Library)

anesthetic in the 1840s, making both doctors and patients more willing to consider surgical remedies.

Finding it difficult to obtain operating privileges in the tightly controlled world of New York hospitals, Sims decided to establish a new hospital for treating women surgically. Financial support for the hospital came mainly from Peter Cooper and a small group of other wealthy New York men, who formed the initial board of governors. However, the organizing drive for the hospital was provided by a group of women, who were leaders of New York society.

Although women such as Mrs. William Astor and Mrs. Peter Cooper (both clients of Parsons) played more visible roles on the original board of lady managers, Sims's success in founding the hospital was largely due to the social prestige and persuasiveness of Sara Platt Doremus. The wife of a wealthy merchant, Mrs. Doremus not only helped Sims gain strong support from influential women, she and her fellow managers oversaw the efficient administration, patient comfort and charitable purpose of the new hospital.

Appealing to the New York State Assembly in 1856 for public support of the new hospital, one advocate chose words and images that were sure to persuade the male legislators to provide funds: He reminded them that, "the wife may be born down with untold miseries, growing out of the marital relation; and the mother, giving birth to her offspring, often sustains such horrible lacerations and injuries as to make her life unbearable . . ."

The Woman's Hospital in the State of New York (the formal title) was incorporated in 1857 and proceeded to grow steadily in numbers of patients and staff over the next ten years. After receiving a grant of $50,000 from the state legislature, the hospital moved to a larger facility located on an entire block of land donated by New York City, which had been a potter's field and is now the site of the Waldorf-Astoria Hotel.

In 1872, Parsons agreed to join his friend and mentor, Peter Cooper, on the board of governors despite the demands of his law practice, Cooper Union and other commitments. He may have been motivated to aid the Woman's Hospital because of the physical and emotional toll that child-bearing was taking on his wife. Between 1857 and 1875, Mary Parsons gave birth to eleven children, five of whom died under the age of five.

He quickly discovered that there was discord between the lady managers and the medical board over a number of issues but especially over the admission of cancer patients. Matters came to a head in early 1874 when Sims refused to follow the directions of both the managers and the governors to cease admitting cancer patients, because of the extra care they required. He also resisted rules limiting the number of visiting physicians attending surgeries. Continuing conflicts with the lay boards coupled with a lack of support from his fellow surgeons on the medical board finally caused Sims to resign in December 1874.

Policy differences and other board conflicts continued even after the departure of Sims, who was succeeded as chief surgeon by Dr. Thomas A. Emmett. In his memoirs, Emmett wrote that there was a great deal of intrigue and "wire pulling" that went on at the hospital, beginning around the time of Dr. Sims's resignation. Emmett recalled a meeting at which a vote was being taken by the board to fill a surgical position. When Parsons nominated a candidate, one of the other board members asked, "But don't you know that he is a Jesuit?" Parsons's answer was, "Why, I always heard he was a surgeon."

Sims returned to the hospital in 1881 as a senior consulting surgeon after developing a successful private practice in the United States and Europe as well as serving as head of the American Medical Association (1876–77). The medical board initially backed Sims's renewed efforts to admit cancer patients, but the majority of the lady managers again resisted strongly.

Like many people at the time, including some doctors, the opponents feared that cancer was contagious, and argued, moreover, that it was more expensive to treat cancer patients than other illnesses. In March of 1882, the majority of the medical board agreed to continue prohibiting cancer cases in order to preserve harmony among the boards. A short time later, Sims resigned again from the hospital and never returned (he died in November 1883).

In his 2013 doctoral thesis, published online by Columbia University ("From Sin to Science: The Cancer Revolution in the Nineteenth Century"), Lawrence Koblenz, MD, gives valuable background on this important period. He speculates that Sims had been invited to return to the hospital "not only because of his international fame and surgical prowess, but, perhaps more importantly, because he had powerful dissident sympathizers on the Ladies' Board and the Board of Governors who agreed with his stance on cancer." Principal among those sympathizers were Parsons and two of the lady managers: Charlotte (Mrs. John Jacob) Astor and her cousin, Elizabeth (Mrs. George) Cullum.

Much of the information about what happened next at the Woman's Hospital as well as details about the founding of the New York Cancer Hospital have been buried in hospital archives. However, the careful research of Dr. Koblenz has uncovered the complex story of what he rightly calls the "intrigue and devotion that even the most wealthy and influential philanthropists needed to bring to bear in a traditional world where power was personal and cancer was taboo."

According to Koblenz, on March 5, 1883, Charlotte Astor summoned her husband's personal attorney, John E. Parsons, to the Astor residence to discuss an urgent matter. She asked Parsons to make an anonymous offer on her behalf to the Woman's Hospital of $170,000. Parsons learned that Mr. Astor was willing to donate that amount if the board agreed to build a separate pavilion on the grounds of the hospital that would be used solely for the treatment of cancer cases.

When the anonymous offer was presented by Parsons, it drew strong opposition from a number of the lady managers and was debated at a series of board meetings over several months. With approval of Mr. and Mrs. Astor, Parsons tried various compromises, such as eliminating the word "cancer" from the name of the pavilion and banning all incurable cases. Parsons and the Astors then decided to call on Dr. Sims for support, but, instead of advocating the addition of a cancer pavilion at Woman's Hospital, he wrote a letter to the boards of the hospital in September 1883, saying:

> A cancer hospital is one of the great needs of the day, and it must be built. We want a cancer hospital on its own foundation-wholly independent of other hospitals . . . There should be a department for men and another for women. Its medical board ought to be men who go into it with zeal, determined not only to give temporary relief to human suffering, but also to do something towards discovering better methods of treatment . . . The subject of cancer is too large

and its interests too great to be lodged in a pavilion subsidiary
to any other hospital, whether special or general.

Although the medical staff was in favor, a majority of each lay
board voted to reject the Astor gift on the spurious grounds that adding a pavilion for cancer care would violate the hospital's charter and
conflict with its mission of treating diseases that were "peculiar to
women." As his clients directed, Parsons withdrew the Astor offer in
January 1884, stating that, "The withdrawal of the proposal, it should
be understood, is coerced and not voluntary. I wish to put myself on
record as protesting against the unwillingness to accept a gift of near
$200,000 in the direction of legitimate work."

Mrs. Astor wrote Parsons during these difficult negotiations: "I
am so grateful, dear Mr. Parsons, for the great pains you have taken."
She signed it "Augusta," her familial nickname. Despite their frustration, Mrs. Astor, Mrs. Cullum and Parsons continued their ties with
the Woman's Hospital (Parsons stayed on to become its president in
1889 and continued as its head until his death in 1915). However, the
letter from Sims had provided the incentive and a blueprint for them
to devise a new plan that called for creation of a new and separate
hospital dedicated solely to the treatment and cure of cancer.

An organizational meeting was held in February 1884 at the home
of Mrs. Cullum and her husband, General George Cullum (she was
the widow of one retired Union General and the wife of another). At
that meeting, Parsons accepted the presidency of the new hospital and
his good friend, Morris K. Jesup was elected vice-president. Joseph
Drexel, a partner of J. P. Morgan in the firm of Drexel, Morgan &
Company filled the position of treasurer.

After discovering in 1883 that she was suffering from cancer, Elizabeth Cullum devoted her energy and a substantial portion of her wealth (nearly $200,000) to the new project. She died in September 1884, shortly after the cornerstone was laid for the New York Cancer Hospital (it was renamed the General Memorial Hospital for the Treatment of Cancer and Allied Diseases in 1899, and "General" was dropped from the name in 1916).

At the ground-breaking ceremony, Parsons, speaking both as president of the new hospital and as a continuing governor of the Woman's Hospital, told the assembled guests:

> I had most earnestly and persistently pressed upon the Woman's Hospital to receive this gift, and I was ignominiously defeated. I was routed, and, because, unfortunately, I could not array on my side of this question those without whom my success was impossible—I mean the women. But there could be no better vindication of the effort to help cancer sufferers, and perhaps of the wisdom of the Woman's Hospital in its rejection of the proposed gift, than what we witness now.

The new building of the New York Cancer Hospital, on Central Park West at 106th Street, was designed with four large round towers on the theory that patients should be housed in circular wards so that contaminated air could circulate more freely and dust would not get trapped in corners. Cancer was still widely considered to be contagious even within the medical profession. The December 1887 issue of *The Medical Record* contained an article on the opening of the Cancer Hospital, which was followed by an article discussing the possible contagiousness of cancer. It concluded with the statement that the principal known causes of the disease were "age, melancholia, syphilis and gout."

Charlotte Astor died of cancer just a week before the hospital opened, so neither she nor Elizabeth Cullum was able to benefit medically from all of the work and financial support they provided. Parsons had both of them in mind when he said at the opening:

> It has often been remarked of discoveries or inventions which have greatly benefitted the human race, that the idea has developed into success in different minds almost at the same time . . . The origin of our hospital illustrates this in a small way. In recent years, the disease has come very near to many homes in our midst, has touched many who were dear to us; and yet the establishment of this hospital is the first effort in this country at an attempt for the exclusive treatment and cure of cancer.

Initially, the hospital only admitted female patients, but in 1888, John Jacob Astor pledged an additional $150,000 in honor of his wife to build a pavilion for male patients, which was opened in 1891 on an adjoining site at 105th Street. Its seventy beds doubled the capacity of the hospital.

Parsons's skills as a legal counselor and trusted adviser had helped guide Mr. and Mrs. Astor in making their large and enlightened gifts to Memorial Hospital. He was also successful in achieving major gifts for the Woman's Hospital from Mr. and Mrs. Russell Sage, but it was a much longer process. Olivia Sage had joined the Woman's Hospital board of lady managers in 1870 and was one of the first women elected to the board of governors when it was reorganized in 1886.

Although her husband was an extremely wealthy financier and railroad baron, Russell Sage was notoriously uncharitable (often called a "miser" and "skinflint" by the press). For many years, contributions by the Sages to the Woman's Hospital were so small that in the annual report of 1895 their cumulative contributions over twenty-five years totaled less than $500.

Nonetheless, there was great respect for Mrs. Sage on the board, especially among the female members, because of her intelligence and many years of hard work. After Parsons became president in 1889, he recognized her value to the hospital by seeing that she was elected a vice-president. He also managed to persuade Russell Sage to join her on the board of governors in 1891.

Within a year, Parsons and the board began discussing plans to move the Woman's Hospital to a site on Eighth Avenue between Ninety-second and Ninety-third streets. They also started discussions to sell its existing property on Park Avenue to the New York Central Railroad in order to escape the constant noise and dirt from the trains that ran along the adjacent tracks. Approval by the Board of Aldermen was required for any sale by the terms of the original gift of the land, so Parsons also led protracted negotiations with the city before reaching a deal.

Speaking at the hospital's annual meeting in 1894, Mrs. Sage referred favorably to the planned new location of the hospital at Ninety-second Street. However, when it became apparent that the board did not have the money to carry out its plans she favored erecting a new building on the existing site of the hospital.

The disagreement worsened when Parsons and the majority of the board decided to move the Woman's Hospital to a location opposite the newly completed Cathedral of St. John the Divine between 109th and 110th streets on Amsterdam and Columbus avenues. At one point, Mrs. Sage threatened to resign, but Parsons told the board, "You could no more shake her away from this hospital, than I can pull the sun down from the heavens." Apparently, Parsons succeeded in mollifying Mrs. Sage, since she agreed to head the building fund campaign.

In an interview by the *Times*, reported shortly before the annual meeting of 1899, she said, "I am now interested in raising money for the Woman's Hospital. We need $400,000 before we can begin the new building. We have been getting subscriptions this past summer, and when that is done, I do not know what I shall devote myself to . . . We now have $325,000 . . . and all of it came to me by check or I made personal calls to get it all, with the exception of one donation. And we have all of this money without applying to an Astor, a Vanderbilt or a Gould . . ."

According to a biographer of Olivia Sage, Ruth Crocker, her husband then suddenly agreed to donate $50,000. Then, after she had told the board of the pledge, Russell Sage just as suddenly withdrew the offer. Eventually, Crocker says, he was shamed or otherwise pressured by two of his wife's friends into fulfilling his $50,000 pledge. In 1904, Mrs. Sage retired from the board at the age of seventy-six, and thus was not involved with the hospital when it reopened in 1906 at its new uptown location. When Russell Sage died in 1907, she inherited his entire fortune of about $70 million.

At her death in 1918, the residue of her estate was divided into shares for many academic and charitable institutions, most of which were valued at $800,000. However, she had provided that a small number of double shares (worth $1.6 million) would go to organizations she cared most about, including the Woman's Hospital. Parsons's careful cultivation of the Sages had produced handsome returns.

His fundraising talents only got better as he grew older. In 1902, his client, Arabella Huntington, made a gift of $100,000 to the Memorial Hospital in memory of her husband, railroad magnate Collis Huntington. This important endowment, including subsequent gifts from Mrs. Huntington, was used to establish the Collis P. Huntington Research Fund, the first cancer research fund in the country.

In 1913, Parsons was one of fifteen founders of the American Society for the Control of Cancer (now called the American Cancer Society), and was one of five men who each pledged $5,000 to cover any deficit in its first year. The principal goal of the society was to raise public awareness of scientific facts about cancer in order to improve opportunities to fund research.

Of the many wealthy donors Parsons dealt with over the years, no one was more challenging for him than James Douglas, a mining engineer and metallurgist who had made a fortune in the copper business. For more than two years, Parsons was actively involved in difficult negotiations with Douglas over a plan of major gifts that would significantly change the future of Memorial Hospital.

In January 1912, Douglas gave $100,000 to Memorial and endowed twenty ward beds for clinical research along with a pledge of $5,000 per year for five years to cover any deficits in operating expenses. The hospital agreed to several conditions required by Douglas, including that the head position on the medical board of the hospital be filled by Dr. James Ewing and that Memorial become affiliated with the nearby Cornell Medical College, where Ewing was a professor.

Another condition in the agreement was that Memorial would "formally adopt the plan of devoting the entire resources of the Hospital to the field of cancer, meaning study and treatment, when the means for such a change shall be provided." That final clause proved to be critical to completing an additional gift of $350,000 offered by Douglas in April 1913.

In making that offer, Douglas believed that his total gift of $450,000 would constitute "the means for such a change." Therefore, a key condition of the new gift was that patients suffering from cancer and allied diseases would be assigned all the ward beds and given precedence in the private rooms. Although the board approved the new gift and terms at the April meeting, Parsons and others continued to be concerned that the return on the increased endowment would not make up for the loss of income from non-cancer patients.

Some board members, however, were willing to risk running short-term deficits in order to save the gift and, in their view, return the hospital to its original focus on cancer research as well as treatment. There were significant differences voiced by board members about the intentions of the founders, including one who contended that "experimental therapeutics and research might not have appealed to the Founders."

The board secretary, Dr. William Coley, summarized his views in a memorandum:

While most of us have felt that this departure from the original purpose of the Hospital was largely brought about by the conditions that then obtained, e.g., lack of interest in the study of cancer and difficulty in maintaining the Hospital as a purely cancer hospital, I believe we have all been looking forward to the time when sufficient endowment could be raised to restore the Hospital solely to cancer work.

Parsons made several attempts to reach a compromise, but in early November, Douglas formally withdrew his offer in a letter, stating: "Your hesitation convinces me that the officials who now control the Hospital will not throw themselves into the research work that I have in view." The stalemate lasted until April 1914 when it was finally resolved with some concessions on both sides.

The major breakthrough was an agreement (and victory for Parsons) that the hospital would treat as many patients as its income and medical and surgical support would permit. If deficits resulted, the board had to cover them through donations rather than from the endowment or reduce expenses (mainly ward patients) in line with actual revenue.

In the end, Douglas gave more than $600,000 to Memorial Hospital. Included in that amount was the value of his personal holdings of radium (3.75 grams worth approximately $375,000), which Douglas turned over to the hospital between 1914 and 1917.

The long negotiation had been an ordeal for everyone involved, but at the age of eighty-five and less than a year before his death, Parsons had helped set Memorial Hospital on a course to becoming the most prestigious cancer center in the country, if not the world.

Chapter Eleven

A Knickerbocker

In his 1872 book, *Lights and Shadows of New York Life*, James McCabe wrote that New York's society was led by "those who claim precedence based on their descent from the original Dutch settlers and style themselves 'old Knickerbockers.'" Parsons was a descendant of one of the pioneering families of New Netherlands, while his wife traced her lineage to an early governor of Pennsylvania and a U.S. senator from New Jersey. Together, they were firmly established as members of that old New York social world portrayed by Edith Wharton so memorably in *The Age of Innocence*.

Unlike that novel's protagonist, a dilettante lawyer named Archer Newland, Parsons had neither the time nor taste for many of the society rituals, especially during the earlier years of his career and marriage. However, he and Mary were a regular part of the social scene at opera performances, first at the Academy of Music and later at the Metropolitan Opera House.

A mutual love of music, which they discovered during their courtship, turned them into patrons of grand opera. In 1853, a group of wealthy men formed a corporation to build the Academy of Music opera house in the fashionable neighborhood of Fourteenth Street and

IN THE METROPOLITAN OPERA-HOUSE—SCENE FROM DIE MEISTERSINGER.

The Metropolitan Opera, 1895 (courtesy of New York Public Library)

Irving Place, near Union Square. Completed a year later, it was one of the largest opera houses in the world and was also home to the New York Philharmonic Orchestra.

Over the next three decades, the Academy remained a cultural icon for the wealthy and fashionable members of New York society. Its importance for that world was highlighted by Wharton in the opening lines of *The Age of Innocence:* "On a January evening of the early seventies, Christine Nilsson was singing in *Faust* at the Academy of Music in New York."

Hinting at the cultural and social battles to come, Wharton continued, "Though there was already talk of the erection in remote metropolitan distances, 'above the forties,' of a new Opera House, which should compete in costliness and splendor with those of the great European capitals, the world of fashion was still content to reassemble every winter in the shabby red and gold boxes of the sociable old Academy. Conservatives cherished it for being small and inconvenient, and thus keeping out the 'new people' . . ."

August Belmont, a wealthy Jewish financier and patron of the arts, was made head of the Academy's board in 1878 in an attempt to improve its financial management, but control over the eighteen boxes was still held by families with names like Astor, Beekman, Livingston and Schuyler. According to opera-world lore, a lawyer representing William Vanderbilt offered to purchase a box at the Academy for $30,000. When the offer was not accepted, Vanderbilt joined with other frustrated opera patrons from both the old and new guard to build a competing opera house when they formed the Metropolitan Opera Company in 1880.

The first president of the company was James Roosevelt, an uncle of Theodore Roosevelt, who was succeeded by George G. Haven, a good friend of Parsons, with whom he shared a box (number 25) at the Metropolitan for many years. When Haven died in 1908, the *Times* noted that, "as president of the Metropolitan Opera and Real Estate Company, he has probably done more for grand opera in New York than any other man. It was his social prestige and experience that handled the delicate situation of allocating Metropolitan Opera House boxes, without favoritism, so successfully."

The new opera house opened on October 22, 1883, with a performance of the still popular *Faust*, starring none other than Christine Nilsson. As reported in the *New York Herald*, "The scene was undeniably beautiful. The three circles of boxes . . . were three 'glittering horseshoes' of as much glory as could well be shown in evening dress and jewels. Diamonds flashed like stars, and the gay tints of hundreds of the most artistic costumes made the three lines perfect pictures." In planning the new opera house, the board made sure there would be enough boxes to go around, so 120 of them were constructed in three tiers, including the famed "Diamond Horseshoe," where tiaras and necklaces were most on display.

Among the notable members of the audience at the opening was Lord Chief Justice John Duke Coleridge, the head of England's judiciary. He was there with Parsons and other leading lawyers following a dinner held in his honor by the bar association. The next night, Parsons hosted a dinner party for the Chief Justice at his residence on Thirty-sixth Street, just around the corner from the Madison Avenue home of J. P. Morgan. During his two-month tour of the United States, Coleridge had also stayed with Parsons at his country home in Lenox.

John and Mary Parsons far preferred private dinner parties to the more elaborate affairs that filled the New York society calendar during the winter season. Beginning in the 1880s, however, they entered more fully into the world of formal balls and tea dances as their daughters (Mary, Edith, Helen, Gertrude and Constance) each reached age eighteen, the socially accepted time for a young lady to make her debut.

The first step in the process of "coming out" into New York society for a young lady was to learn the art of being a hostess. In his book, *Impressions and Experiences,* William Dean Howells described one of the customs that Mary Parsons would have imparted to her daughters:

> Certain ladies receive once a week throughout the season; others receive on some day each week of December or January or February, as the case may be . . . There is tea or chocolate or mild punch and a table spread with pastries and sweets, which hardly any one touches. A young lady dedicates herself to the service of each urn and offers you the beverage that flows from it. There is a great air of gayety, a very excited chatter of female voices, a constant flutter of greeting and leave-taking and a general sense of amiable emptiness and bewildered kindness when you come away.

The Parsons girls, like Edith Wharton and others of their sex and social class, received little formal schooling, but they were exposed to art, history, culture and even current events by their parents at home and during travel abroad. To prepare them for their expected futures as wives and mothers, it was important for them to become skilled in the practical art of shopping for their households and themselves.

An English author, Iza Duffus Hardy, wrote of her visit to New York in the 1880s in *Between Two Oceans: Or Sketches of American Travel*:

> Fourteenth Street especially is the headquarters of ladies bent on shopping, and at certain hours and seasons it is so thronged that it is a very slow progress one can make . . . It is a perfect bazaar; not only is there a brilliant display in the windows of everything good to look at, from exotic flowers to encaustic tiles, and everything one could possibly wear, from Paris-imported bonnets to pink satin boots, but the side-walk is fringed with open-air stalls, heaped high with pretty things, many of them absurdly cheap.

The tradition in New York's polite society had long been for a daughter to be introduced to an assembly of family and close friends at a party in the family home. By the time Edith Jones (later Wharton) was ready to make her debut in 1879, there was a growing trend to hold debutante parties at Delmonico's and other fashionable public spaces, but her mother's friend, Mrs. Levi Morton, offered to give the party at her home on Fifth Avenue. In her autobiography, *A Backward Glance*, Edith recalled her unhappy entrance into society:

> I was therefore put into a low-necked bodice of pale green brocade . . . my hair was piled up on top of my head, some friend of the family sent me a huge bouquet of lilies-of-the-valley, and thus adorned I was taken to a ball at Mrs.

Morton's, in Fifth Avenue . . . Houses with ballrooms were still few in New York: almost the only ones were those of the Astors, the Mortons, the Belmonts and my cousins, the Schermerhorns. As a rule, hostesses who wished to give a dance hired the ballroom at Delmonico's restaurant; but my mother would never have consented to my making my first appearance in a public room, so to Mrs. Morton's we went. To me the evening was a long cold agony of shyness.

A high point of each social season was the series of Patriarch Balls, which were run for many years by Ward McAllister. In 1873, he founded the Society of Patriarchs, initially a group of twenty-five "representative men of worth, respectability, and responsibility," each of whom, as subscribers, was entitled to invite "four ladies and five gentlemen" to the balls. In his memoir, *Society as I Have Found It,* he wrote that the secret of success for the balls was to make it "extremely difficult to obtain an invitation to them and . . . to make them a stepping stone to the best New York society . . ."

The first Patriarch Ball of the 1885–86 season was held on December 29, 1885, at Delmonico's where the ballroom was decorated with an arrangement of electric lights and flowers. The *New York Times* reported that among the highlights of the ball were the appearance of Mrs. William B. Astor, "who has always been considered the chief patroness of the Patriarchs' balls," and the installation of J. Pierpont Morgan as a Patriarch. Listed among the guests were "Mr. and Mrs. John E. Parsons and Miss Parsons" (their daughter, Helen, would have been a debutante that season).

Of the many balls that Ward McAllister staged over the years, none was more elaborate than the New Year's Ball of 1890, which was held at the Metropolitan Opera House. According to the *New York Herald*, McAllister planned "to enlarge society and bring in twelve hundred in place of four hundred," and the invitation list "shows how admirably Mr. McAllister has succeeded in expanding his four hundred. It is made up of millionaires, bankers, lawyers, merchants, dandies and nobodies." The invitation listed one hundred forty-four men as subscribers in alphabetical order, beginning with William B. Astor and including John E. Parsons.

Unlike the "dandies and nobodies" and some of the idle millionaires on that list of subscribers, Parsons had a demanding legal practice that did not allow him to "sleep in" after a night at the opera or one of the balls. Yet, despite his many professional and civic commitments, he found time to spend occasional evenings with his male friends at one of his clubs or at bar association dinners honoring his fellow lawyers and judges.

He particularly enjoyed attending dinners, lectures and art shows at the Century Association, one of the oldest and most prestigious of New York's clubs. Founded in 1847 to promote both culture and good cheer among its members, its constitution provided that its membership "shall be composed of authors, artists and amateurs of letters and the fine arts." From its early days, however, the Century welcomed as members many financiers, industrialists, merchants and leading lawyers like Parsons.

The highlight of each year at the Century was the Twelfth Night Festival, which even a good Presbyterian like Parsons enjoyed to the full. As its fiftieth anniversary report described one of the celebrations: "Following a Middle Age precedent . . . we decorated our walls with holly and green moss; we hung them with antlers and armor and the skins of beasts; we chose our king, the lineal descendant of the legendary three kings of the East . . . and then, preceded by the court jesters, fools and the boar's head, made their stately way to the supper table."

Whether it was a fancy dress ball attended by hundreds or a private party at a residence or club, New York's newspapers competed in reporting on many activities of the social world, including the names of society leaders in attendance on each occasion. Among the most well-read of those articles were reports on the funerals of leaders in the business, civic and social worlds, which identified the honorary pallbearers as well as other notable individuals at the services.

In 1897, an article in the *New York Times* noted that "John E. Parsons is among the well-known faces frequently observed among the general mourners" and observed that "some men are as scrupulous in paying their respects to the dead as they are in other matters of etiquette . . . Their frequent attendance at funerals is indicative of a strong sense of duty as well as their loyal friendship to those whose lives they pay tribute . . ."

Parsons was devoted to his family and close friends with whom he shared the same background and values. In a memorial he composed for his close friend George deForest Lord, Parsons wrote in 1893: "It is the boast of our country that we have no class distinctions; that all alike may have the opportunity of higher education, and that to all is open the pursuit of a career, and the acquisition of position and fortune. I cannot reconcile myself, however, to think that there are no advantages in gentle birth and careful early training."

Chapter Twelve
Havemeyer and the Sugar Trust

O f the many clients Parsons represented over the years none benefitted more from his legal talents than Henry O. (Harry) Havemeyer. Their professional relationship began during a protracted series of court battles during the 1870s between separate branches of the Havemeyer family over stock in the Long Island Railroad.

After several trials and appeals, Harry Havemeyer retained Parsons to negotiate a settlement, which succeeded in making peace among the warring cousins. Thereafter, Parsons remained the principal lawyer for Havemeyer and his extended family, as well as their many business interests, for more than forty years.

Harry was the third generation of the Havemeyer family to work in the sugar business. In 1876, at the age of twenty-nine, he became the principal partner in the firm of Havemeyer & Elder, whose profits were derived largely from its refinery in Brooklyn. In 1882, the refinery was destroyed by an explosion and fire. Yet, within eighteen months, the firm rebuilt it into what the *Brooklyn Eagle* described as

Henry O. Havemeyer (courtesy of Harry W. Havemeyer)

"the largest of the kind on the face of the globe . . . Soon there were 650 ships a year tying up at the Havemeyer plant to deliver raw sugar. By then, Brooklyn was the source of sugar for two-thirds of the nation as well as a prime source for customers around the world."

Increasing sugar prices and high profits caused others to enter the refining business in Boston, Philadelphia and other cities. With so much of their capital invested and so much profit to be made, Harry and his partners determined that they needed a way to protect them from disruptive price competition. They turned to Parsons to devise a legal structure that would work as well for sugar refiners as the Standard Oil Trust structure (formed in 1882) had done for John D. Rockefeller and his partners.

Aided by John Dos Passos (a corporate lawyer and father of the novelist) Parsons crafted a form of commercial trust, which functioned as a new type of business organization. As Alfred S. Eichner noted in *The Emergence of an Oligopoly: Sugar Refining as a Case Study*, this arrangement made it possible to get around the common law prohibition against holding companies and enabled important information about the trust to remain a secret, since, unlike a corporation, it did not have to obtain a state charter.

In 1887, the Sugar Refineries Company (commonly known as "the Sugar Trust") was formed when a number of independent refining concerns combined and transferred their assets to the trust in exchange for trust certificates. Each participant's capital interest in the trust was determined by a formula for assessing the asset value and capacity of the various refineries

To be effective, it was important to have most of the major sugar refiners participate in the trust. As owners of major refineries, the

Havemeyers became the principal promoters of the trust strategy, but it took nearly a year before the deal was finally signed. While overseeing compliance with the legal and regulatory requirements, Parsons was also involved in the negotiations with a number of refinery owners.

Most of the independents joined the trust readily, seeing an economic advantage. Others agreed because they feared the consequences of remaining outside the combination. However, Joseph B. Thomas, a Boston refinery owner, was reluctant to participate because Harry Havemeyer was known to be a difficult and domineering person. According to a Havemeyer family memoir, Thomas told Parsons that he considered Harry Havemeyer to be "a brute," but he eventually relented and joined the board.

Parsons served from the outset as general counsel for the Sugar Trust and was elected as one of the eleven trustees. Theodore Havemeyer, Harry's brother, was the titular head of the board, but Harry was chairman of the mercantile committee. In that role, he controlled all the key decisions in setting prices, controlling production and determining the profitability of the operating companies. He relied heavily on John Searles, the secretary and treasurer, but in the view of Charles P. Norcross, a journalist who wrote a series of articles about the Sugar Trust, "Next to Henry Havemeyer, Parsons was the most important person in the Sugar Trust."

Harry Havemeyer testified before a Senate Committee in 1894 that the principal object in forming the Sugar Trust was to control the price and production of sugar in the United States, and that making profits was incidental to that control. At its inception, it controlled more than seventy percent of all domestic sugar production, but its market share later rose well above ninety percent.

Only a few months after the Sugar Trust became operative, a New York Senate committee began hearings into trusts operating in various industries, including the Standard Oil Trust, whose head, John D. Rockefeller, was one of the witnesses. Harry Havemeyer, who spent several days testifying about the Sugar Trust, was advised by Parsons not to disclose the specific terms of the trust agreement, arguing that they were private and outside the scope of the hearings. When pressed by repeated questions about the agreement from members of the committee and its counsel, Parsons responded: "I once had an opinion that there would be no objection to showing that agreement to anybody . . . but since [Attorney] General Pryor, the counsel of your committee, has declared that this investigation proceeds against people who have committed a crime . . . I prefer to base my declination upon all legal points."

After concluding that there was no evidence of criminal activity, the New York Attorney General filed a civil lawsuit in November 1888, claiming that the trust arrangement operated in restraint of trade under the common law of the state. A newspaper account of the trial noted that "John E. Parsons, who drew the trust agreement under which all the mischief about sugar has been done, appeared for the North River Sugar Refining Company" (one of the Sugar Trust's refiners that was a New York corporation).

As disclosed by Parsons many years later in a congressional hearing, the lawsuit was a test case initiated by the Tammany Hall political leadership, who wanted to demonstrate their opposition to monopolies through a well-publicized trial. At the same time, the Sugar Trust board members wanted to ascertain, as Parsons put it, "whether what they had done was right, and if not, establish what was right and conform to it; and they desired to have the case heard before a judge who would go as strongly in that direction as possible."

The trial judge decided against the Sugar Trust in what Parsons described as "a luminous opinion," by which he probably meant that the judge had clearly identified the right issues for the appellate court's review. The case was ultimately decided in June 1890 by the New York Court of Appeals, which ruled only that the North River Company had violated its corporate charter by renouncing its power of independent action and, therefore, the trust had to be dissolved.

Compounding the problems facing the Sugar Trust in the summer of 1890 was the newly enacted Sherman Antitrust Act, a federal law that prohibited business combinations and monopolies from restraining trade in interstate commerce. Passed by the Senate by a vote of 51 to 1 and unanimously by the House of Representatives, the Sherman Act became law on July 2, 1890. Many commentators have since noted that the broad language of the legislation that gained such overwhelming support for its enactment also led to serious problems in judicial interpretation and government enforcement.

Perhaps in recognition that the Sherman Act was about to become federal law, the Court of Appeals declined to rule on whether the Sugar Trust was an illegal combination or monopoly under state law. Instead, the court concluded that, "it becomes needless to advance into a wider discussion over monopolies and combinations and restraint of trade and problems of political economy. Our duty is to leave them until some proper emergency compels their consideration . . ."

The decision necessitated a major reorganization, so Parsons engaged Elihu Root, a leading corporate lawyer, to assist him in transforming the trust structure into a holding company. They also advised the board to incorporate in the business-friendly state of New Jersey, which allowed a holding company to own stock in other corporations. It took the lawyers about six months to complete all the legal work necessitated by the reorganization, but on January 11, 1891, the *Times* reported: "The Sugar Trust dropped out of the financial world yesterday, and the American Sugar Refining Company rose up in its stead."

Still known as the Sugar Trust, the new company proceeded to add four Philadelphia-based sugar refiners to its holdings in 1892, giving it effective control of almost ninety-eight percent of the nation's sugar refining business. The public outcry over the widening spread of such monopolistic practices forced the newly re-elected president, Grover Cleveland, to demonstrate that his administration would vigorously enforce the Sherman Act.

Even though the Standard Oil Trust was a more widely known example of what many considered an abusive monopoly, Cleveland's new attorney general, Richard Olney, chose to make the Sugar Trust the target of the government's first major antitrust case. There is evidence that neither Cleveland nor Olney was eager to enforce the Sherman Act aggressively and probably selected the Sugar Trust because preliminary legal proceedings had already begun before they took office in 1893.

The case was filed in May 1892 in the U.S. Circuit Court at Philadelphia. American Sugar Refining Company and its four most recent corporate acquisitions were named as defendants, but the case made history under the name of only one of the acquired companies with the title, *United States v. E. C. Knight Co.* Parsons wisely retained as his co-counsel a noted Philadelphia attorney, John G. Johnson, who was not only a highly respected leader of the bar in Pennsylvania but was also renowned for his skills as an advocate in both trial and appellate courts.

Born the son of a blacksmith, Johnson did not attend college, but after clerking in a law firm, graduated from the University of Pennsylvania Law School. A fellow lawyer described Johnson as "a huge man with an intense gaze, sweating at every pore, with both hands extended . . . driving home points like spikes into a tie. He jammed meaning into words, and his sentences were surcharged. His speeches were as rapid as they were brief."

The key issue in the *Knight* case lay in the language of the federal statute, which Parsons and Johnson addressed very simply in their initial written answers to the government's bill of complaint: "We aver that our said contract was not within the provisions of the Act of Congress of the 2nd of July, 1890 [and] that it did not concern commerce . . ." Parsons and Johnson made a telling point in the trial court, which eventually persuaded the Supreme Court, namely that manufacturing, even though the products eventually enter or indirectly affect interstate commerce, was not covered within the statute.

In January 1894, the trial judge decided in favor of the Sugar Trust, finding that:

"The contracts and acts of the defendants relate exclusively to the acquisition of sugar refineries and the business of sugar refining in Pennsylvania. They have no reference and bear no relation to commerce between the States or with foreign nations. Granting, therefore, that a monopoly exists in the ownership of such refineries and business, (with which the laws and courts of the State may deal) it does not constitute a restriction or monopoly of interstate or foreign commerce."

An appeal was quickly made by the government to the Circuit Court of Appeals, which upheld the trial court in March 1894. Anger over the decisions in the *Knight* case added to widespread attacks on the Sugar Trust at the time for using its influence in Congress to gain favorable tariff treatment. A story in the *New York World* on March 3, 1894, headlined "Gigantic Robbery," described the Sugar Trust as a "robber baron that has plundered the people in pursuance of law" and said that it "should be stripped of the [tariff] protection it now enjoys."

The *Knight* case was finally decided in January 1895 when the U.S. Supreme Court ruled against the government in a vote of 8 to 1 (Justice John Marshall Harlan was the lone dissenter). The opinion, written by Chief Justice Melville Fuller, agreed with the lower courts' interpretation of the Sherman Act, finding that manufacturing did not constitute interstate commerce and, therefore the Sugar Trust's combined refining operations were not in violation of the federal antitrust law, adding: "The fact that an article is manufactured for export to another state does not of itself make it an article of interstate commerce . . ."

Commenting on the outcome, The *Washington* (D.C.) *Evening Star* reported on January 22, 1895 that "Attorney General Olney declined to express any opinion on the decision in the sugar case . . . It is known, however, that Mr. Olney has never had any faith in the government's ability to enforce the Sherman Act against the Sugar Trust . . . It is also said that he is equally skeptical of success against the tobacco trust, the whiskey trust, or any of the other great combinations, with the possible exception of that of the railroads."

Jack Simpson Mullins, who wrote a PhD thesis on Harry Havemeyer and the Sugar Trust at the University of South Carolina in

1954 noted that, "The preponderance of professional opinion is that the *Knight* case went to trial in a deplorably weak form and was improperly pleaded by government counsel." He speculated that Attorney General Olney "may have been influenced, consciously or unconsciously, by his corporate leanings" and that, "Grover Cleveland was a reasonably close friend of Harry Havemeyer, a wealthy Democrat . . ." Mullins also acknowledged the flaws in the Sherman Act, which seem to have been the main problem for the weakness of the government's case.

Parsons and his co-counsel had obtained the guidelines from the Supreme Court that were needed to protect the Sugar Trust and other manufacturing combinations like it from running afoul of the Sherman Act. In 1899, President McKinley's attorney general, John W. Griggs, confirmed that the door was still wide open to certain mergers when he stated in a letter that was widely quoted in the press: "All of the companies to which you refer are similar to the sugar combination (that is, monopolies in manufacture) and are not within the jurisdiction of the federal courts."

Acquiescence in the *Knight* decision by both the White House and Congress during the Cleveland and McKinley administrations set off a rash of mergers in corporate America. In the view of historian Naomi R. Lamoreaux, author of *The Great Merger Movement in American Business: 1895–1904*:

> Americans had watched with foreboding the formation
> of Standard Oil, the first "trust," and with increasing anxiety
> the imitations that Standard's success spawned in industries
> as diverse as sugar refining and lead processing. Then, as the

merger movement crested, with hundreds of firms disappear-
ing into horizontal consolidations, it seemed as if the United
States had been transformed overnight from a nation of competing, individually owned enterprises into a nation dominated by a small number of giant corporations.

A laissez-faire attitude toward business was succeeding as much
in Washington as on Wall Street and in the boardrooms of corporations. Harry Havemeyer, Andrew Carnegie and other corporate
titans believed in applying to the business world what some called
"social Darwinism." At a hearing into trusts and combinations held
by the federal Industrial Commission in 1899, Havemeyer was asked
whether a trust represented the survival of the fittest in business. He
replied that he based his entire economic and political philosophy on
that proposition.

Parsons had a less Darwinian view. In testimony before a congressional committee investigating the Sugar Trust in 1911 he said,
"I think, so far as possible, the question is of leaving the American
citizen, one or ninety millions, to take care of himself." But then,
noting that the issue had "assumed public importance and notoriety
recently," he told the committee, "I have invariably and exclusively
put myself on the side of the public. I am a member of the public; I
want my sugar as cheaply as possible . . ."

He based his legal and personal defense of the Sugar Trust on the
rule of reason: that possession of monopoly power in itself was not
illegal. When he was asked in the same hearing about his view of the
efficacy of the Sherman antitrust law, Parsons responded:

> If the Sherman antitrust law means, what the Govern-
> ment contends . . . that two persons who are competing can-
> not become partners and, in that way prevent competition
> between themselves, without violating the Sherman antitrust
> law . . . it means ruin for the industries of this country. I do
> not think that was what was intended. You have to enforce
> the law as the extremists on one side claim, or you have to rec-
> ognize it as interpreted by the Supreme Court of the United
> States, by reading into it . . . the rule of reason.

Citing John Stuart Mill in support of his views, he went on to say,
"The larger the scale upon which business is done, the cheaper can the
commodity be sold. All political economists say so. It is the experience
of all merchants, manufacturers and business men that it is so, and
. . . I think it will be the experience of this arrangement that it is so,
consistent with the payment of a fair price for labor."

He also pointed out that as a result of the purchase of the competing sugar refineries, the output of sugar was not diminished, nor was
the average price to the consumer increased. As Benjamin R. Twiss,
a close observer of Parsons's handling of the *Knight* case observed in
*Lawyers and the Constitution: How Laissez-Faire Came to the Supreme
Court*: "Although such an argument was a far cry from the free market
of Adam Smith, it was quite consistent with contemporary American
laissez-faire theory, and is another illustration of how the bar brought
that theory to the Supreme Court."

Parsons endured extensive questioning in the hearing that lasted
over several days, patiently answering one congressman after another.
At one point, however, fatigue and frustration caused him to give the

terse but revealing answer: "What I say is, Federal Government, hands off, because I am a States-rights man. I thought our Constitution was based upon that idea, and I thoroughly object to the modern idea of having the Federal Government solve all the problems of the country."

Theodore Roosevelt set forth a very different view when he wrote in his 1913 autobiography: "Among the big corporations, even when they did wrong, there was a wide difference in the moral obliquity indicated by the wrongdoer . . . The Supreme Court in its decree dissolving the Standard Oil and Tobacco Trusts, condemned them in the severest language for moral turpitude; an even severer need of condemnation should be visited on the Sugar Trust."

The conflicting views of Parsons and Roosevelt are still being debated. In an essay written in 1961, which is still widely quoted, Alan Greenspan gave a free-market perspective on the damage done to the U.S. economy in the wake of the Sherman Act:

> To sum up: The entire structure of antitrust statutes in this country is a jumble of economic irrationality and ignorance. It is the product: (a) of a gross misinterpretation of history, and (b) of rather naive, and certainly unrealistic, economic theories. As a last resort, some people argue that at least the antitrust laws haven't done any harm. They assert that even though the competitive process itself inhibits coercive monopolies, there is no harm in making doubly sure by declaring certain economic actions to be illegal.
>
> But the very existence of those undefinable statutes and contradictory case law inhibits businessmen from undertaking what would otherwise be sound productive ventures. No

one will ever know what new products, processes, machines, and cost-saving mergers failed to come into existence, killed by the Sherman Act before they were born. No one can ever compute the price that all of us have paid for that Act which, by inducing less effective use of capital, has kept our standard of living lower than would otherwise have been possible.

Greenspan then added: "No speculation, however, is required to assess the injustice and the damage to the careers, reputations, and lives of business executives jailed under the antitrust laws." This strong criticism was remarkably similar to a response by Parsons to the Congressional committee in 1911 when pressed for his opinion of the Sherman Act: "It was monstrous that men are being criminally indicted under a law over which the Supreme Court puzzled for four months before they could decide what it meant." As was well-known to the committee members, Parsons was then a defendant in a criminal action brought by the federal government under the Sherman Act against directors of the Sugar Trust.

Chapter Thirteen
Return to Lounsberry

B y the time he reached age sixty, Parsons had become one of the most acclaimed lawyers in the country, and his income was among the highest in the legal profession. An article in the *Times* about top-earning lawyers described Parsons as an "adviser to big corporations and estates," who is "believed to have the finest legal practice in the country."

According to the *Times*, Parsons was "reputed to have received one of the largest fees ever taken by a lawyer when he drew up the charter of the Sugar Trust, receiving $400,000 for this service. As general counsel for the Trust, he defended it during the attack on the combination and that defense is said to have added another $100,000 to his fortune."

Although the fees that the *Times* reported in its widely publicized article may have been exaggerated, Parsons's income allowed him to maintain a very comfortable lifestyle. In New York City, he lived in a substantial residence on East Thirty-sixth Street, just a block from J.P. Morgan's brownstone on Madison Avenue.

In the fashionable resort town of Lenox, Massachusetts, he owned a large house as well as a separate working farm. Beginning in the

Lounsberry (courtesy of Rye Historical Society)

1870s, country life in the Berkshires provided him a refuge in the summer months from the demands of his law practice and board commitments. However, he wanted an additional place closer to New York where he could retreat with his family on weekends and for other escapes from the city.

His preference was to find a place in Rye, the small community in New York's Westchester County where he had spent much of his youth. Several members of his family still lived there, including his brother, William, who had inherited a large home built by their maternal grandfather, Ebenezer Clark. Parsons's search ended successfully in 1893 when he was able to purchase Lounsberry and return to his boyhood home. It had been owned since 1858 by his uncle, James H. Parsons and was occupied after the death of James by his widow.

A description of the property in the National Register of Historic Places states that, "Lounsberry . . . has a Greek Revival Main Residence. The oldest visible portion of the house was built by Edward Lamb Parsons in 1838 and incorporates within it an earlier structure standing on the land when he purchased it in 1831. Of gray painted wood with white trim, the imposing residence is three stories high, eleven bays wide, and three bays deep on a stone foundation. The main (west) facade is dominated by a two-story portico with fluted Ionic columns with Scamozzi capitals supporting a triangular pediment. Doric pilasters accentuate the corners and set off the bays of the building's main block and the north and south wings.'"

Set back from the Boston Post Road (the original colonial mail route between New York and Boston) the house was surrounded by more than thirty acres of fields and woodland that ran down to a salt marsh and a harbor on Long Island Sound. In 1893, the neighboring property to the south was owned by the family of the recently deceased Dr. John Clarkson Jay, a grandson of John Jay. On the north side was the estate of Joseph Park, who was head of Park & Tilford, grocers to New York City's carriage trade.

As the distinguished Columbia historian Kenneth Jackson wrote in *Westchester, The American Suburb*: "Later in the nineteenth century, as the 'robber barons' of American finance and industry began to amass fortunes on a scale previously undreamed of in human history, Westchester County became the first large suburban area in the world to develop. The most famous of the new brand of baronial edifices were intended as weekend or summer retreats for the families of New York's wealthiest men . . ."

The Village of Rye was then just a hamlet, consisting mainly of a residential section with a small shopping district and a railroad station. In her book, *Fifty years of Rye: 1904–1954*, Marcia Dalphin described some scenes of the village as it would have looked around the turn of the century, including "a quaint, low-lying white house that was once the Strang Inn, where in 1704 Madam Sarah Knight on her horseback journey from Boston to New York spent the miserable night recounted in her journal . . ." Further on was "Herman Wagner's Saddlery Shop and Cushion's Blacksmith Shop." She noted that even in 1906, there were only thirty automobiles registered to residents of Rye.

Soon after he returned to Lounsberry, Parsons joined with Joseph Park and other leading residents who opposed decisions being made by the Rye Town Board that threatened the quality of life in the village. To make their opposition more effective, they formed the Rye

Village Protective Association and named Parsons as its president as well as its legal counsel.

The association's first priority was to defeat an application by the Port Chester Electric Railway Company to run a trolley line from Port Chester to Mamaroneck through the Village of Rye, with a branch line to Rye Beach, a popular public attraction on the shore of Long Island Sound. The battle became newsworthy enough for the *Times* to run an article about a contentious hearing held in Port Chester in May 1896, which included this succinct summary of the issues:

> Many of the residents of [Port Chester], which is a manufacturing place, believe that in justice to the common demands, Rye should be opened to trolley roads. The chief landowners are as firm in their belief that the splendid highways of this town should not be given up to the use of any corporation . . . Joseph Park, it is said, expends from his private purse . . . $7,000 a year in keeping the highways in proper condition. The Rye roads are among the finest in Westchester County.

The battle between the business interests in Port Chester and the Rye property owners continued for nearly four years. Parsons spent a great deal of time and effort appearing *pro bono* at hearings before road commissioners and judges. In leading the opposition, however, he was motivated by much more than the threat that trolleys posed to the value of his property on the Boston Post Road. Summing up his case at one of the commission hearings in 1899, Parsons stated that he had known Rye all his life and that the proposed trolley line would "destroy the character of the place."

Eventually, a compromise was reached, allowing the trolley company to run a line through the village's business district to Rye Beach. In return, the company agreed to a route that ran along a road beside the railroad tracks to Mamaroneck instead of down the Boston Post Road. When construction of the line through the village business district commenced, the *Port Chester Journal* commented: "Of course there are some people who object to the extension, others object to the change of routes and some who want no trolley at all. But one might as well try to stem the Falls of Niagara as to prevent the introduction of a trolley road in the present century."

In the midst of the "trolley war," as it was dubbed by the newspapers, Parsons and a number of other Rye residents had to contend with another type of damage to their properties. It was bizarre enough to receive widespread press coverage, including these excerpts from an article in the *Kansas City Journal* on August 22, 1897:

> The millionaires of Rye, on the Sound . . . have combined to keep George Myers, the religious sign painter out of their life. . . . This George Myers travels around the country on an antique bicycle, to which are slung pots of paint. The truly religious Mr. Myers wears a Salvation Army uniform. Whenever he arrives in a neighborhood he thinks peculiarly wicked he dismounts, chooses a rock, or a stone wall, or, in a pinch, even a board fence, and on this, with lightening-like rapidity, he paints, in large letters, a text or warning to evil-doers . . .
>
> John E. Parsons, the celebrated lawyer, has a fine country place at Rye. Mr. Parsons is a good church man, and it really

grieved him to look out his window one fine morning and see on his stone fence, in letters two feet tall: "Repent or go to ——." Having painted the "to," it was plain that the enthusiastic Mr. Myers had arrived at the end of the fence and had no more canvas, so to speak . . .

There exists at Rye a protection association. John E. Parsons is president of the association, which moved against Myers. When Reginald P. Sherman met him on the highway, Myers had already painted "Seek sal——" on a rich man's fence when Mr. Sherman tapped him on the shoulder. "Get out of here just as fast as that wheel will carry you or to jail you go for trespass." Myers jumped on his bike and disappeared. The texts will be promptly erased and the scenery around Rye will resume its wonted aspect.

Not long after the trolley war was settled, Parsons faced yet another threat to Lounsberry because of plans to construct a second railroad line through Rye. The first railroad reached Rye in 1849, and soon thereafter its steam-powered trains were running frequently between New Haven and New York City. Through a series of mergers and acquisitions, the New York, New Haven and Hartford Railroad (known as the "New Haven") grew rapidly, and by the turn of the century, it had absorbed more than twenty-five other lines.

Despite the New Haven's success, a new corporation, named the New York and Port Chester Railroad Company, applied for a franchise to run an electrified railway from New York to Port Chester along tracks to be laid close to the shore of Long Island Sound. Descendants of John Jay reached an agreement for a right of way over part of the historic Jay property, but Parsons refused to have the tracks run through his land. His objections forced a hearing before the State Railroad Commission in November 1901.

According to the *New-York Tribune*, a witness at the hearing testified that "the road would cut the estate of John E. Parsons in two, and I don't think any amount of money would compensate him for the damage caused to his estate. With Mr. Parsons, there is a great deal of sentiment about this as his father had the estate before him, and Mr. Parsons can afford to have sentiments of this kind." Eventually, the competing railroad was taken over by the New Haven, thereby ending another threat to Lounsberry as well as to the quality of life in Rye.

There were other conflicts, however, between residents of the village and the town officials. The *Tribune* reported in August 1897 that "more than two hundred residents from the Village of Rye descended on the assessor's office in Port Chester to press their grievances over the recent tax assessments of their properties. The total assessment for the Village had been increased to $15.5 million from $3.7 million the prior year . . . The streets for several blocks were crowded with vehicles and coachmen in livery, and the assessors soon realized that they would have to deal with some of the wealthier residents . . . among the well-known residents present or represented by counsel were John E. and William H. Parsons, who are assessed for more than $70,000 in personal taxes."

Tax fairness was only one of the issues dividing the wealthy part-time residents and year-round inhabitants in many of Westchester County's suburban communities. Despite disparities in wealth within the Village of Rye, the shared opposition to actions of the Rye Town officials helped to bind the residents together in a common cause with the creation of the Rye Village Improvement Association.

Formed in 1894, its stated goal was improvement and beautification of the village. The association was among a growing movement of civic improvement groups around the country that were modelled on the Laurel Hill Association in Stockbridge, Massachusetts, which began in 1853. Parsons was very familiar with the movement and had for many years been a major benefactor of the Village Improvement Society of Lenox, which is located next to Stockbridge.

The Rye Village Improvement Association assumed responsibility to provide various services needed in the village, such as watering the dusty streets, constructing sidewalks and planting trees. When the association decided that the village was not receiving adequate police protection from the town, it organized a village police force consisting of a chief and two patrolmen. To finance its activities it relied on donations from a growing number of residents, but it also held summer fairs, including one in 1900 held on the grounds of the American Yacht Club that attracted more than one thousand people.

A major step in advancing Rye's village improvement occurred in 1903 when John and William Parsons joined with their cousin, John Whittemore, to preserve an historic structure in the heart of the village. After purchasing the building, widely known as the "Square House," and saving it from destruction, they donated it to the village as a museum with relics of Rye's colonial history. Dating to about 1730, it had long been operated as a tavern whose patrons included George Washington, John Adams and the Marquis de Lafayette.

The gift of the Square House was made in memory of their grandfather, Ebenezer Clark, who had instilled in them a strong sense of community service and civic philanthropy. It also held fond memories for the three cousins, who had all been educated in the building when it was used as a school house by their uncle, Samuel Berrian, sixty years earlier.

When renovations were completed a year later, the Square House became the municipal building for the newly incorporated Village of Rye. The New York Legislature passed a bill authorizing incorporation, followed by a special election held at the meat market owned by Theodore Fremd, a long-time village leader. On September 12, 1904, the village taxpayers voted 155 in favor, 47 opposed, giving village residents greater control over their government through home rule.

The Rye voters also elected William Parsons as the first president of the new Village Board of Trustees. As a memorial to her husband after his untimely death, his widow gave to the village a large amount of land surrounding the Square House for use as a village green. To that gift she later gave a parcel of adjoining land as the site for a new library. Completing the improvements by the Parsons family to the village center, John Parsons built a small brick apartment building with an arcade next to the Square House.

Parsons's home at Lounsberry was close to the border of Harrison and Rye. The same was true of the home of his next-door neighbor, Joseph Park, who had laid a road through his property (now called Park Avenue), which took him directly to the Harrison train station for his commute to New York City. It appears that the need for a school house for the new Union Free School District of Rye and Harrison motivated Parsons to donate the necessary funds.

At the ceremony for the laying of the cornerstone in 1897, Parsons, in his brief comments reported in the local newspaper, stated:

"For our own welfare, and for the welfare of the nation, it is necessary that the foundation of these children's character be built in true knowledge." As one later graduate of the Parsons Memorial School in Harrison has expressed, "It must have been a very emotional day for Mr. Parsons, whose wife of some 40 years had passed away the previous year, to dedicate the school to his first three (of 11) children all of whom had passed away 30–35 years prior—all under the age of five!"

Chapter Fourteen

Tariffs and Other Challenges

In the frequent reporting and commentary about the Sugar Trust, Parsons was often cited for his skill as an architect of the trust concept as well as for winning the *Knight* case in the Supreme Court. His testimony before a congressional committee in 1912 was covered by many newspapers around the country, including the *Omaha Daily Bee*, which reported: "Mr. Parsons modestly explained . . . that whatever credit or blame is due for the combination of the sugar interests must fall on him and not Henry O. Havemeyer. Whereupon, Representative Madison exclaimed, 'Aha, at last we have discovered the real father of the trusts.'"

Parsons received much less notoriety, however, for skillfully guiding the Sugar Trust through the legal, legislative and political minefields of federal tariffs. In the view of Jack Simpson Mullins, whose doctoral thesis probed deeply into the Sugar Trust's history, "No other single factor influenced the fortunes of the Sugar Trust as much as the protective tariff."

By the time the Sugar Trust was formed in 1887 the American sugar refining industry had benefitted from tariff protection for almost one hundred years. Even when Congress introduced a relatively low

The Trusts (courtesy of New York Public Library)

tariff on the large imports of raw sugar used by domestic refiners, their profitability, though volatile, was still protected by a higher tariff on imported refined sugar.

Harry Havemeyer made a memorable claim in a congressional hearing that, "The mother of all trusts is the custom tariff bill." He candidly told the committee members: "Without the tariff I doubt that we should have dared to take the risk of forming the trust. It could have been done, but I certainly should have not risked all I had . . . in a trust unless the business was protected as it was by the tariff."

The Sugar Trust faced a major challenge in 1890 as Congress debated provisions of the McKinley Tariff, named after then Ohio Representative (later President) William McKinley. Of all the items under review, the sugar tariff was the most important, because it produced the largest amount of revenue for the federal government at a time when there was great political pressure to reduce the budget surplus. Political dealmaking was intense as the House and Senate hammered out the final terms.

When signed into law, the McKinley Tariff law set higher duties on manufactured goods and lowered them on some grades of refined sugar, but it put raw sugar on the duty-free list and compensated domestic sugar growers with a subsidy roughly equal to the former tariff. Although the Sugar Trust failed to get all that it wanted, the combination of duty-free raw sugar imports and its dominant share of the market enabled it to greatly increase its annual profits in the following years by as much as $10 million (some estimates run as high as $30 million) annually.

The favorable outcome for the sugar refiners was due in large part to their effective lobbying work, which was headed by John Searles, secretary and treasurer of the Sugar Trust. Ida Tarbell, a noted muck-raking journalist, claimed in her 1911 book, *The Tariff in our Times*, that the victory for the Sugar Trust and other protectionists "firmly established the politico-industrial alliance . . . and that alliance had found the Congressional leader it needed—a man who was willing to accept its dictates and to fight for them . . . and who took as a matter of course that he and his party would receive in exchange what financial and organizational aid they required."

That man was Senator Nelson A. Aldrich, who, as chairman of the Senate Banking Committee, was such a solid supporter of the Sugar Trust's interests in Congress that the press nicknamed him the "sugar senator." Others called him the "Senator from Havemeyer."

As a partner in a wholesale grocery firm before entering politics, Aldrich became a close friend of Harry Havemeyer, who helped educate him about the economics of the sugar business. One of his Senate colleagues, John Ingalls of Kansas, once confessed that Aldrich was one of the few legislators who could discuss intelligently a subject "so inextricably confounded that . . . nobody in the Senate understands it."

Maintaining good relations with their political allies and preparing for the next round of tariff reforms became top priorities of the Sugar Trust's senior management. The Trust's board resolved that, "all matters pertaining to tariff legislation be . . . referred to the president [Havemeyer], the treasurer [Searles] and Mr. John E. Parsons, with full power to take, in their discretion such action as they may think best for the interest of the company."

Grover Cleveland was reelected president in 1892 on a pledge to reduce tariffs. In his second term, he appointed John G. Carlisle, former Speaker of the House of Representatives and an expert on tariffs, as secretary of the Treasury. As the new tariff worked its way through Congress in early 1894, Carlisle worked closely with an industry committee consisting of his long-time friend Havemeyer as well as Searles and Parsons.

The House of Representatives voted for moderate reductions in tariff duties, but the Senate voted for higher schedules on many items, including one that favored the Sugar Trust. The resulting Wilson-Gorman Tariff Act of 1894 fell far short of Cleveland's goals, but, after calling it a product of "party dishonor," he let it become law without his signature.

It was of great importance to the Sugar Trust to help assure the reelection of their political allies, especially Senator Aldrich, who was then the senior Republican member (and later chair) of the Senate Finance Committee. In order to accomplish that goal they carried out a carefully planned program of political contributions and lobbying.

At the time, there were no legal restrictions on the lobbying activity of individuals or corporations nor on their campaign contributions to candidates or party organizations. Also, U.S. senators were elected by state legislatures rather than directly by voters until adoption of the Seventeenth Amendment to the Constitution in 1913, so much of the campaign finance money was spent at the state level.

Havemeyer testified at a U.S. Senate committee hearing in 1894 that the Sugar Trust never gave money for the purpose of influencing legislation. However, he admitted it contributed to both parties in state contests depending on the party in power, and received "a good deal of protection for our contribution." Parsons testified that the only presidential campaign contribution of which he was aware was $10,000 to one of Benjamin Harrison's campaigns.

The committee was investigating charges that the Trust's campaign contributions to various senators during the 1892 election amounted to bribery. It was triggered by articles published in the *New York Sun* and *The Press,* a Philadelphia newspaper, alleging that bribes had been paid to certain senators by the Sugar Trust to influence the next round of tariff reforms (eventually passed as the Wilson-Gorman Tariff Act of 1894).

According to the newspapers, when the Democratic members of the Senate Finance Committee were meeting, they were joined by Secretary of the Treasury John G. Carlisle, who was quoted as saying: "Gentlemen associated with the sugar-refining interests . . . subscribed to the campaign fund of the Democratic Party in 1892 . . . several hundred thousand dollars, and at a time when money was urgently needed . . . I trust you will prepare an amendment to the bill which will be reasonable and somewhat satisfactory to those interests."

During the Senate hearing in 1894, Havemeyer was asked to produce the Sugar Trust's records of political campaign contributions, but on advice from Parsons, he declined to do so. His refusal led to an indictment of Havemeyer by a grand jury in the District of Columbia for contempt of the Senate investigating committee, threatening him with a fine and possible imprisonment.

Because of delays, Havemeyer did not go on trial until May 1897. To assist him in his defense, Parsons again retained John G. Johnson, his co-counsel in the *Knight* case, as well as Nathaniel Wilson, a leading Washington DC lawyer. As one newspaper noted, Havemeyer "was represented by a brilliant array of counsel."

In his final argument, the lawyer for the Senate committee noted that a newspaper had quoted a Sugar Trust director as saying that

"We own the Senate body, boots and breeches; brain, morals and all."
Therefore, he argued that it was the duty of the committee to investigate the Trust's contributions to elections involving senators even at
the local level. Havemeyer's counsel countered that the committee's
inquiry was not pertinent to any possible legislation and was unautho-
rized prying into the private affairs of a citizen.

The *Times* reporter covering the trial wrote: "There was almost a
breathless atmosphere in the courtroom when the court reconvened at
1 o'clock. The room buzzed with speculation as to what the decision
would be. Just before the judge entered, a bright little girl ran over to
Mr. Havemeyer and said she wanted to shake his hand. The millionaire sugar king took her in his arms and kissed her. He then put her
down, and she ran back to her mother. 'I don't know who the girl is,'
said Mr. Havemeyer to his attorney, Mr. Parsons, 'but I think it is a
good omen.'"

The judge then granted the motion of the defense to dismiss the
case against Havemeyer and instructed the jury to enter a verdict of not
guilty, saying, (as reported in the *Times)* "Any corporation has a right
to make campaign contributions, unless it is shown that the money has
been used for corrupt purposes. I do not think the Senate investigating
committee had any right to inquire into the private affairs of individuals, and doing so was beyond the power of the Senate."

The final report of the Senate investigating committee found no
conclusive evidence of bribery but noted that the members "strongly
deprecate the importunity and pressure to which Congress and its
members are subjugated by representatives of great industrial combinations, whose enormous wealth tends to suggest undue influence,
and to create in the public mind a demoralizing belief in the existence

of corrupt practices." Two of the committee members wrote an additional condemnation of the Sugar Trust for its "thoroughly corrupt form of campaign contributions, being given to two opposing political parties . . ."

Despite this harsh criticism, the Sugar Trust achieved its goals in the tariff reforms, and, with the skillful advice of Parsons, neither the company nor any of its senior management had been penalized. However, other serious problems and more difficult legal battles were yet to come.

In 1906, the government filed multiple criminal charges against the Sugar Trust, which carried a total fine of $2.2 million. Securing 156 indictments, the U.S. attorney general alleged that the Trust had received illegal rebates from various railroad companies in violation of the Elkins Act, a law passed in 1903. Rather than negotiate a settlement, Parsons chose to litigate the first case, adding Joseph Choate to the defense team because of his experience with railroad rebate cases.

Parsons challenged the indictments on the grounds that the alleged crimes took place prior to the passage of the Elkins Act. Despite the impressive array of defense lawyers, the jury found the Sugar Trust was guilty on the basis that the rebates were paid after the law was in force. Parsons then advised the company to settle all the charges for a fine of $200,000, about half of the potential maximum penalty.

In less than a year, the Sugar Trust was in greater trouble, charged with customs frauds that involved large sums of money due the government over a period of many years. The fraud was revealed in November 1907 when customs agents raided the Trust's plant in Brooklyn. They discovered that the scales had been rigged to reduce the weight of raw sugar being unloaded off a ship from Java.

The burlap bags filled with sugar were weighed on seventeen separate scales to determine the amount of money due to the seller as well as the customs duties owed to the government. When evidence was found that the Trust's employees had adjusted the springs of each scale through small holes, resulting in short-weighting, it became known in the press as "the case of the seventeen holes."

Both civil and criminal cases were successfully prosecuted by the U.S. attorney for the Southern District of New York, Henry L. Stimson, assisted by a team that included Felix Frankfurter, recently graduated from Harvard Law School. To avoid further litigation and bad publicity, the Sugar Trust agreed to settle the customs fraud case for $3 million, including fines already paid, or roughly one-third of the total amount sought by the government from the Trust.

Some lower level employees were indicted and tried separately for criminal involvement. When the general superintendent of the Brooklyn refinery was charged, the newspapers reported that the government was at last on the trail of officials "higher up in the company."

None of the corporate officers or directors of the Sugar Trust was ever implicated or charged with knowledge, let alone involvement, in the custom frauds. However, the widespread publicity surrounding the disclosure of the "seventeen holes" took its toll on Harry Havemeyer, who died in 1907, two weeks after the raid on the Brooklyn docks.

Attorney General Wickersham stated in the Annual Report of the Department of Justice for the 1910 fiscal year that, "the evidence adduced indicates that this company, down to minute details, was virtually run by one man, and that its executive management during the period of the frauds was in the entire hands of the president, Henry O.

Havemeyer, assisted by the secretary and treasurer." It is noteworthy that Parsons's name was not on the Attorney General's black list.

In his 1913 autobiography, former President Theodore Roosevelt wrote with pride about the work of his administration on these cases: "We had already secured heavy fines from the Sugar Trust . . . for unlawful rebates. In the case of the chief offender, the American Sugar Refining Company (Sugar Trust), criminal prosecutions were carried on against every living man whose position was such that he would naturally know about the fraud . . . The evidence showed that the president of the company, Henry O. Havemeyer, virtually ran the company and was responsible for all the details of management. He died two weeks after the fraud was discovered . . ."

It may have been Roosevelt's not-so-veiled indictment of Havemeyer that motivated Parsons to write the following memorandum, which was found among his papers at his death:

> With respect to the charges, or further innuendos, in which my name is used or suggested with respect to frauds upon the Custom House . . . I have to say that never, until I received communication from Mr. Havemeyer . . . did either knowledge or suspicion come, directly or indirectly, to myself, or, so far as I know, to the late Mr. H. O. Havemeyer or any other associate of mine in the board of directors, that there was undervaluation of sugar imported by the company or any withholding from the government of anything due it, or any collusion between the company and Government employees.
>
> When Mr. Havemeyer first told me that such a charge had been made, it was, as I understood, his direction—and it

was my advice—that every record which the company had on
the matter be offered to the Government. And this was done.
So far as I know, it is not claimed that anything was withheld
and certainly nothing was withheld with my knowledge.

During the years since I became a director . . . the impor-
tations of the company have been enormous; the total of
duties actually paid have been hundreds of millions of dollars.
With the details of this and of all the other vast business of
the company, it is obviously impossible that I, as counsel or
as director, should be familiar, and the same was true of the
other directors . . .

This statement will, I think, be accepted by those who
have known me since nearly sixty years I began my active
personal and professional career in this city—a career which,
it is not, under the present circumstances, unfit to say, had,
for many years before I became a member of the Sugar Trust
board, been well and widely and even conspicuously known
to my brethren at the bar and my fellow citizens . . .

Chapter Fifteen
Lenox and Country Life

A delay in Harry Havemeyer's trial for contempt of Congress allowed Parsons to spend much of the summer of 1896 at his country home in Lenox, Massachusetts. He and Mary had first visited the small village in the Berkshire Hills during their honeymoon in 1856, but they did not start spending family vacations there until 1871. It was then still largely a farming community and had not yet become one of the most fashionable resorts of the Gilded Age, when it was often called the "Newport of the Mountains."

In his 1948 book, *The Last Resorts*, Cleveland Amory offered a theory that, "generally speaking, the following groups have come to the social resorts in this order: first, artists and writers in search of good scenery and solitude; second, professors and clergymen and other so-called 'solid people' with long vacations in search of the simple life; third, 'nice millionaires,' in search of a good place for their children to lead a simple life . . . ; fourth, 'naughty millionaires,' who wished to associate with the 'nice millionaires' but who built million-dollar cottages . . . dressed for dinner, gave balls and utterly destroyed the simple life . . ."

Amory's theory applied particularly well to the evolution of Lenox

Stonover Farm (courtesy of Jonas Dovydenas)

as a social resort. Richard S. Jackson, Jr., and Cornelia Brooke Gilder, authors of *Houses of the Berkshires: 1870–1930,* note that families who came from New York and Boston to the Berkshires in the 1870s were looking for a simple country life away from the urban heat and grime. In addition to the clean mountain air, they were drawn there by the scenic beauty that had previously attracted Herman Melville, Nathaniel Hawthorne and Fanny Kemble as well as other artists and intellectuals.

The Rev. Henry Ward Beecher helped spread the word about Lenox and the joys of Berkshire country vacations in his book *Star Papers*, writing that city dwellers would become "transcendentally happy" in the country. In an entry for July 1854, he wrote: "Eagerly we escaped from the glow and rage of town-heat, as if we had been escaping from a burning city . . . thus we sped on from station to station, the hills growing larger all the time until we reached Lenox . . ."

At first, Parsons and his family stayed in a local hotel, but in 1872 he had sufficient funds to buy a large property in collaboration with two friends: Henri W. Braem, the Danish consul in New York, and Dr. Richard C. Greenleaf, a Boston physician. They divided the land into three separate parcels and agreed to position their houses so that each would have an unobstructed view of the Berkshire countryside. At that time, Parsons was still one of Amory's "solid people," but he was on the verge of becoming one of the "nice millionaires."

In 1875, Parsons built a mansard-roofed home, called "Stonover," on Yokun Avenue near the village center, to which he made substantial additions ten years later. Until the 1870s, most Berkshire country houses were modest wooden structures. The peak building years were from the 1880s to 1920s as increasing wealth generated larger and more elaborate mansions. Stonover was among the earliest of these so-called "cottages" that wealthy families from New York, Boston and elsewhere built in Lenox from the end of the Civil War until the start of the Great Depression.

Constance Cary (Mrs. Burton) Harrison, a popular author and playwright during the Gilded Age, spent many summers in Lenox. In her *Recollections Grave and Gay*, she describes how the resort changed over time:

> When we first went to Lenox, the lovely hill-village had not parted with its old-time characteristics of unpretending hospitality. The people who we met there, summer after summer, were of the cultured and refined class of American society, knowing each other intimately and satisfied to exchange simple entertainments in their pretty, picturesque homes . . .
>
> I lived there long enough to see a mighty change. The rural hill-sides and pastures, bought up at fabulous prices, were made the sites of modern villas, most of them handsome and in good taste. The villas were succeeded by little palaces, some repeating the facades and gardens of royal dwellings abroad . . . Stables were filled with costly horses, barnyards with stock bearing pedigrees longer than their owner; the dinner hour moved on to eight o'clock, and lastly house-parties, "weekends," and the eternal honk and reek of the motor-car.

The grandest of all the cottages was "Shadowbrook." It was built in 1894 on 900 acres at a prime hilltop location for Anson Phelps Stokes, a successful mining and real estate investor. The palatial mansion, containing one hundred rooms, held the title of the largest private residence in America until it was bested a year later by "Biltmore," George Vanderbilt's home in North Carolina. Andrew Carnegie later bought the house, and died there in 1919. Stokes was a good friend and neighbor of Parsons both in Lenox and New York and gave special mention in his memoir to "John E. Parsons, the eminent lawyer," praising him for stopping the *New York Herald* from publishing a stolen photo taken of guests at Stokes's home.

Morris Jesup, a close friend of Parsons, was another millionaire who built his cottage on a hill with a commanding view of the Berkshire countryside. Parsons had first met Jesup when he boarded in the Jesup home while he was a student at NYU in the 1840s. Joseph Choate, Parsons's great friend and frequent legal adversary, chose to build his home, called "Naumkeg," a few miles away in Stockbridge. Ever the wit, when he was asked why he chose that location, he replied: "In Lenox you are estimated; in Stockbridge, you are esteemed."

In Lenox, Parsons could satisfy a taste for rural life that he inherited from his father, who, as Parsons once wrote, "had an Englishman's love of the country." Soon after building Stonover, Parsons bought a separate farm property of approximately 700 acres, where, in 1890, he built what a local newspaper described as a "commodious" farm house with steep gables. It also had a large barn that housed a herd of Jersey cows, which Parsons proudly showed at the local agricultural fair. When he was asked at the start of a congressional investigation of the Sugar Trust in 1911 to state his age and occupation, he replied that he was more than eighty years of age and, having retired from law practice, considered himself to be a farmer.

In 1904, the *New York Times* reported that the total assessed valuation of property in Lenox was $4.7 million. Listed among the highest assessments were George H. Morgan (brother-in-law of J. Pierpont Morgan) at $160,000, John Sloane (W&J Sloane Furniture) at $136,000, George Westinghouse (industrialist) at $96,000, Morris Jesup (banker) at $94,000 and Parsons at $82,000. The relatively low assessment shown for Anson Phelps Stokes of $57,000 was because the bulk of his property was located over the town line in Stockbridge.

The overall tax burden on the cottagers increased substantially after 1913 when the federal income tax was reinstituted after ratification of a constitutional amendment. However, it was due to Joseph Choate's skills as an advocate that the Supreme Court had ruled the prior income tax unconstitutional in 1895, prolonging the good times for him and his ilk. In addition to the tax burden, maintenance of these large residential and farm properties required a retinue of men and women, and most of the population of the town was dependent for a living on the income from working or providing services for the cottagers.

Almost every estate had its rustic garden house, lily pool and beds for annuals and perennials that were displayed when the growers competed for prizes in July at the annual exhibition of the Lenox Horticultural Society. The *Times* did not exaggerate when it reported one year that, "There is no event of the season in which Lenox society shows more interest or takes more pride than its mid-summer flower show. The deep-seated rivalry to show a better bloom in sweet peas or asters, a more glorious color in a gladiola or a more perfect specimen of a phlox excites the Lenox villa owner even more than to see his hunter take a round of five-foot hurdles without clipping a timber."

Although the laurels really belonged to the estate gardeners, the owners, both women and men, were credited with the prizes in the society pages. Even on vacation Parsons and Choate continued to compete through their gardens, both winning prizes for their flowers and vegetables. One issue of the *Times* reported that, "Mrs. Edith Wharton, the novelist, made a sweeping victory in the class for the best annuals and perennials" while "Mrs. John E. Parsons won the prize for the best figs and the best collection of vegetables."

The gardens at Edith Wharton's home, "The Mount," were among the most admired in Lenox. She collaborated on the design of the gardens and landscaping with her niece, Beatrix Farrand, who subsequently received landscaping commissions from other cottagers. In a letter to her friend (and lover), Morton Fullerton, Wharton wrote, "Decidedly, I am a better landscape gardener than novelist, and this place [The Mount], every line of which is my own work, far surpasses the *House of Mirth.*"

In addition to the horticultural society, Lenox cottagers organized one of the earliest garden clubs, which even antedated the Garden Club of America. One society column reported that "at the recent Lenox Garden Club meeting various topics were discussed, including one on 'Weeds,' presented by John E. Parsons." He was also one of the founders of a farmer's club, formed for the promotion of agriculture and farm management. Among the lectures attended by Parsons and other owners of large estates was a discussion on the extermination of rats.

Following the example of the Laurel Hill Association in Stockbridge, the first village improvement society in the country, cottagers and townspeople formed the Lenox Association to care for the streets, parks and overall appearance of the town. Parsons was one of its earliest and most generous supporters, opening part of his property to the public for walks and picnics and later donating funds for a park in the center of the town.

His attachment to Lenox grew so strong that when his daughter Helen died of typhoid fever in April 1892 at age twenty-four, he chose to have her buried there rather than with three of his other children who were buried in Rye. As a memorial to Helen, Parsons donated a chapel, called St. Helena's, in the nearby farming community of New Lenox where he had long supported a Sunday school. When the cornerstone was laid in the summer of 1892, the *Pittsfield Sun* reported that "the chapel is being built of grey stone from the east mountain and will probably be the finest in the country."

Inspired by his experience with New York tenement children as head of the Brick Church's Sunday school, Parsons began another project in Helen's memory. Through Morris Jesup, he became interested in the mission of the "Fresh Air Fund," which Whitelaw Reid, publisher of the *New-York Tribune*, was then actively supporting. In 1893, Parsons bought property along a stream near Lenox and turned what had been a small country hotel into St. Helen's Home for Fresh Air children. From July to September each year for more than twenty years, he paid all expenses for roughly 500 boys and girls from New York City's tenements to spend two healthy weeks in the Berkshires.

Although he was a staunch Presbyterian there was no church of that denomination in the Lenox area, so he and his family attended the local Episcopal Church. A note published in an 1898 issue of *The Triangle*, a NYU magazine, commented that "John E. Parsons is an Elder of the old Brick Presbyterian Church of this city for six months of the year, and for the other six months he is a Warden of

Trinity Episcopal Church at Lenox, Mass., thus securing two chances for making his calling and election sure."

A *New England Magazine* article in 1900 stated that, "the church is visited by pilgrims from far and wide; for few cities can boast churches of greater beauty." The same article offered another reason for the church becoming a stop on a sightseeing tour: "At the Lenox Episcopal Church in the summer one can see more wealth represented than in any other church in the land, lest it be Trinity in Newport."

The Episcopal Church in Lenox was especially important for Mary Parsons, who died in August 1896 after a short illness (probably meningitis). After a family gathering at Stonover, the funeral service was held at Trinity Church, followed by interment in the Parsons family lot, next to Helen. A delegation of eighteen Fresh Air children from St. Helen's Home attended the funeral.

A *Times* "Society" column in September commented that, "The death of Mrs. John E. Parsons last month will have an effect upon the season and will, of course, keep a large family out of society there. Mrs. Parsons had been so long identified with Lenox and had been so universally beloved there that many of the cottagers feel a personal sense of loss in her death."

As a memorial to his wife, Parsons gave Trinity Church a parish house, which was completed in 1898. Constructed of native bluestone, it was designed to resemble a small Norman church. His gift of $35,000 also covered all of the furnishings, including a grand piano. In his brief remarks at the dedication, he said that the gift was a memorial of one who loved the parish and the people.

After his wife died, it gave Parsons great comfort to have his three unmarried daughters—Mary, Gertrude and Constance—with him at

Stonover (Constance married in 1908, but Mary and Gertrude never married). Edith often visited with her children and husband until they separated in 1905, while Herbert and Elsie spent many vacations with their children at Stonover farm.

The younger generations enjoyed a growing array of sporting and recreational activities over the years. In 1890, the *Times* noted that "the principal amusement was driving, with buckboards the favorite carriage because of its adaptation to country roads. Other vehicles, such as surreys, victorias, wagonettes and, occasionally, four-in-hand coaches are used for shorter drives. Riding is interesting the younger people, and among the best equestriennes are the daughters of John E. Parsons, who are out every day."

The following year, Parsons became an original shareholder in the Mahkeenac Boating Club at the Stockbridge Bowl (also called Lake Mahkeenac). Black bass fishing was a favorite sport at the club with teas and dances at the boathouse enjoyed throughout the season

Over time there was a gradual lengthening of the Lenox season, which reached its height in September and October when a number of cottagers escaped the stormy coastal weather of Newport and Bar Harbor to enjoy the fall colors in the Berkshires. A highlight in September was the parade of floral tubs (a British term for a carriage), described by an enthusiastic reporter for the *Boston Evening Transcript* in 1897:

> Excursionists and all-the-year-round residents have shared in the excitement caused by the "tub" parade, and were cheered by the sight of all the nobby, flower-laden vehicles and the sound of martial music at the parade. The floral

festival at Lenox is a beautiful thing. Each cottager at this aristocratic place agrees to decorate all the carriages in his stable and bring out all his horses . . . The leader is always a young and beautiful girl. This year it was Miss Sloane [who] drove a small village cart, entirely covered with flowers, even to the spokes of the wheels, and overhead hung a great flower parasol . . .

Parsons regained a fuller life in Lenox after his marriage to Mrs. Florence V.C. Bishop in March of 1901. Rather than take a trip abroad on their honeymoon, they spent much of the spring in Lenox, where she also had a large estate called "Interlaken." In June, the *Times* noted that they "were seen out frequently on horseback as they both enjoy this method of viewing the fine scenery of the Berkshire hills."

In September, its social columnist reported that, "The autumnal season at Lenox is now in full swing, starting with coaching parties going to the County Fair in Pittsfield; John Parsons and several others rode over on horseback; coming up are the annual floral 'Tub' Parade, horse show events, and the golf tournament the last week in October."

At age seventy-two, Parsons was clearly both an accomplished rider and fit enough to make the roundtrip ride of more than fifteen miles from Lenox to Pittsfield. A few years later, his daughter, Gertrude, was unhurt when she was thrown from her horse while riding in the Berkshire Hunt, a drag over eight miles of rough bottom, stone walls and wire fences. Less fortunate was Anson Phelps Stokes, who had to have a leg amputated after it was crushed in a riding accident on his estate.

The Parsons maintained an active social life at some of the dinners, lawn parties, musicales, dances and other entertainments that filled the calendar throughout the season at Lenox. They also hosted a number of family members and friends as houseguests at Stonover as well as such distinguished visitors as Lord Chief Justice Coleridge of England and Baron von Munn, the German Ambassador.

If he needed some peace and quiet, he could retreat to the Lenox Club, a male bastion where he served for many years as a governor. He was also especially interested in the Lenox Library and served as its president for twenty years. This favorite town resource was housed in a stately Greek Revival structure with Ionic columns and an elegant cupola. It was built in 1815 as the Berkshire county courthouse and became the home of the public library in 1874. Among the many Lenox residents who served on the board with Parsons were Edith Wharton and his daughter, Mary.

When Parsons died in 1915, his obituary in the *Berkshire Eagle* called him the "foremost cottager of Lenox as regards his interest in the town and its environs." He was buried with his wife Mary and daughter Helen in the Church on the Hill burying ground. It is likely that he would have agreed with another cottager who said, "We live a life which is the nearest approach to English country life of any place in America. When we come up to Lenox, we come for the quiet of the hills and the beauty of country living."

Chapter Sixteen
Family Matters

Failing to uphold its claim of publishing "All the news that's fit to print," the *New York Times* included the following item in its "What is Doing in Society" column on March 2, 1901: "In this column, engagements are announced with authority . . . Rumors, unless well founded, are seldom noticed . . . This rumor is given as a *rumor* only. The interested parties are said to be Mrs. Florence Van Cortlandt Field Bishop, the widow of David Wolfe Bishop and Mr. John E. Parsons. Mr. Parsons is a widower, and, like Mrs. Bishop, has lived in the Berkshire Hills in the summer, where he has his country seat."

The *Times* continued in much the same gossipy vein when it covered their wedding less than two weeks later, describing the bride as "quite young and hardly looks as if she has reached middle age" (she was then fifty while Parsons was seventy). The article mentioned her old-New York ancestry (the Van Cortlandts and Fields) as well as the substantial fortune she had inherited from her late husband, which, it added, "comes largely from the older Lorillards." It also noted that "Mr. Parsons, the celebrated lawyer, has been the family lawyer and legal adviser of Mrs. Bishop."

Three generations of Parsons (courtesy of David Parsons)

The wedding in the chantry of Grace Church in Manhattan was attended only by family members. Herbert Parsons and his wife Elsie were there along with Herbert's sister Edith and her husband D. Percy Morgan as well as his three unmarried sisters: Mary, Gertrude and Constance. Also attending were the bride's two sons, David Wolfe Bishop and Cortlandt Field Bishop, together with his wife Amy.

Besides their connection through her family's legal matters, the newlyweds had known each other socially for a number of years both in New York and in Lenox, where they each owned country estates. Despite the difference in their ages, they had many interests in common, including a mutual love of the Berkshires, horseback riding and other pleasures of country life as well as a fondness for European travel.

With three of their children married and the others healthy and independent adults, the senior Parsons might have expected to be relatively free of family worries, let alone scandal, but that was not to be. The first one to cause them concern was David Bishop, who was the subject of a *New York Times* article on September 9, 1901, that began with the headlines: "David Wolfe Bishop Made a Prisoner—Clubman Arrested for Speeding His Racing Automobile."

David, age twenty-six, was charged with driving well above the speed limit of sixteen miles per hour along Seventh Avenue while frightening pedestrians and horses, including one belonging to the president of the Board of Health. After spending several hours in a jail cell, he posted bail and was free to enter the automobile race from New York to Boston that began the next day at the Waldorf Astoria.

He had been introduced to the sport of automobile racing (originally called "automobiling") by his older brother Cortlandt, who had brought a gasoline-propelled tricycle to Lenox in 1897. It was the first automobile seen in the Berkshires, and the local residents christened it the "holy terror." The Town Council quickly decreed that "Any vehicle drawn by other than horse, man, dog, ox or goat must keep one wheel in the gutter" and could not exceed six miles per hour. Cortlandt was also stopped for speeding on Jerome Avenue in the Bronx in 1902.

David, who did not attend college and never worked, moved to France as a young man, where he used his inheritance to purchase a home in Paris as well as a chateau and large estate near Rhein. In December 1911, his brother received a cablegram informing him that David had shot and killed himself in Paris.

Cortlandt Bishop fared far better in life than his younger brother. Although he had undergraduate and law degrees from Columbia, he never practiced law, preferring to use his wealth and social position to promote development of both automobiles and airplanes. As president of the Aero Club of America, he funded and worked closely with the Wright Brothers, Glenn Curtiss and other early aviators in the United States and abroad, leaving his days of automobiling behind. Later on, he became the successful owner of a prominent art gallery.

Parsons also made news because his French chauffeur was arrested twice for speeding in New York City. In March 1907, a headline in the *Times* reported: "J.E. Parsons Angry—Accuses Policeman—Scuffle in Home When Chauffeur is Arrested." What followed in the article was an account that sounded like a comic opera, with the arresting officer running after the chauffeur into the vestibule of the Parsons house, thinking the driver was trying to escape. According to the reporter, Parsons then arrived on the scene and objected to the invasion of his privacy. He was quoted as saying: "The policeman took hold of the chauffeur's collar. I then asked the policeman what he meant by his actions. With that he drew his club and threatened to use it, whether on the unresisting chauffeur or on one of us . . . I do not know."

That case ended with Parsons paying a fine, but just a month before, the *Times* had carried a much less conspicuous article about the arrest of the same chauffeur for speeding in Central Park. According to the report, Parsons told the magistrate that he was in the automobile with some of his family, and that he was sure that the machine was not going at the rate of twenty miles per hour, as testified by the policeman. Parsons also said he believed in the law against speeding and had never sanctioned fast driving. The policeman testified that he had timed the machine over a fixed course but might have been mistaken, and on hearing that statement, the magistrate let the chauffeur go.

The publicity surrounding the multiple speeding tickets was nothing, however, compared to what the family endured during the protracted marital troubles of Edith and Percy Morgan. When the senior Parsons were married in March 1901, the Morgans had been married for fifteen years and had four children ranging in age from six to thirteen. To outward appearances, their family life was harmonious, and Edith was especially happy to be renting a large home next door to Lounsberry, the family property on the Post Road in Rye.

An article in the *New York Tribune* on July 1, 1901 reported:

> The famous old Jay mansion has taken on new life since its occupancy by Mrs. D. Percy Morgan. She has thrown the mansion house open to her friends, and the women of Harrison and Rye meet there in large numbers to carry on charita-

ble work for the poor of New York . . . Mrs. Morgan's father,
John E. Parsons, owns a colonial mansion adjoining the home
of the Jays . . . Nearly a score of the women are associated
in the fresh air work . . . in the last year, the women gave
241 poor women and children of Manhattan an outing at the
sea shore.

Then on May 29, 1904, when Edith and their eldest child were
away from home, Percy Morgan suddenly left with his three younger
children, taking them by train to a rented home in Pennsylvania. As
he later testified in their separation trial, he had hoped to convince
Edith to move with him from the Jay mansion and get away from
the influence of her father, whom he believed to be an insuperable
obstacle to their marriage.

As the *Washington Times* reported, "From May until October,
Percy kept the children at Radnor. Then his handsome wife executed
a sensational move. Going to Radnor in a big automobile she entered
the house, took possession of the children, rushed with them to a
waiting car, and, in an instant later was flying toward the New York
State line with them."

In April 1905, a suit was brought on behalf of Edith against Percy
in White Plains, the county seat of Westchester County, asking for a
legal separation on the grounds of cruelty and desertion. Edith was
represented by Henry W. Taft, who was a name partner in one of the
major New York law firms and a brother of future President William
Howard Taft. Although Henry Taft, a renowned corporate lawyer and
skilled litigator was a good friend of Parsons, it was curious that he
agreed to handle a domestic relations case. His success on behalf of

Edith Morgan, however, may have brought him Mrs. John Jacob Astor as a client when she successfully sued Col. Astor for divorce in 1909.

Taft based his proof of Percy's cruelty mainly on his desertion of Edith but also on his speculating with Edith's investment funds. Edith also claimed that she was undermined by his interfering with her running of the household. When Taft attempted to call some of the servants as witnesses, opposing counsel objected on the grounds that it would just be "kitchen gossip," adding, "If servants could testify against their masters and mistresses, Lord save us, where would we all be?"

In late June of 1905, an article in the *New York Evening World* was headlined: "Court Forbids Morgans to Marry Again" and reported that the decree of legal separation was based on the grounds of Percy's desertion of Edith. It awarded Edith sole custody of the four children, but Percy was granted visiting rights and was not ordered to contribute to the support of Edith or the children. Because Edith and Percy remained legally separated, they managed to avoid the social opprobrium of divorce and even continued to be listed together in the Social Register.

Although Parsons would certainly have wanted to spare Edith the pain and publicity of the lawsuit, he must have been satisfied with the outcome that left her legally separated rather than divorced. He was a strong supporter of the law in New York State, which did not then permit divorce for any reason other than adultery. In a speech to a large inter-church group of clergy and laymen less than a year after the lawsuit ended he praised New York's conservative divorce law and called on other states to adopt legislation that would "preserve the sanctity of the family and purity of the home."

Parsons's strongly held views on marriage and divorce were again challenged within his own family by his daughter-in-law, Elsie Clews Parsons, who had married his son Herbert in 1900. By the time of their marriage, Elsie had already received a PhD in sociology from Columbia and had embarked on a long and distinguished career as a sociologist and anthropologist.

Herbert, who had graduated from St. Paul's School, Yale and Harvard Law School, was a partner in his father's New York law firm at the time of his marriage. Unlike his father, a life-long Democrat who had avoided public office, Herbert had recently entered New York City politics as a Republican Alderman in 1900. He became a close political ally of President Theodore Roosevelt, and in 1904 was elected to his first of three terms in the U.S. House of Representatives. During a congressional investigation of the Sugar Trust's contributions to political parties John Parsons was asked whether he had ever personally contributed to the Republicans. He responded: "That's a personal question. I have a son who does not agree with me, and I do not agree with him, but I may think that he is a better fellow in the House of Representatives than another fellow and for that reason and for personal and family reasons, I have been willing to help his personal campaign. Am I to be condemned for that?"

In 1906, Herbert and Elsie were living in Washington with their two young children when her book, *The Family*, was published, causing widespread shock and criticism. In it, she argued for a more flexible morality, based on sincerity and privacy that included the possibility of trial marriage as well as divorce by mutual consent, along with an increased sense of obligation by parents to their children.

The *Deseret Evening News* of Salt Lake City expressed the view of many across the country (whether they had read or only heard of the book): "Mrs. Elsie Clews Parsons, in her new book, 'The Family,' ventures, if correctly reported, the revolting suggestion that marriages be made probationary before they are made permanent . . ." The *Washington Times* called the book, "The most widely criticized book on record."

A dispassionate critic wrote in *Good Housekeeping* magazine, that, "The noisy advent of Mrs. Elsie Clews Parsons' book, 'The Family,' amid the fiery denunciation from the press and pulpit, [was] precipitated by the publisher's wily trick of advertising it with one sentence concerning trial marriages . . ." While Herbert remained a member of Congress, Elsie used the pen name of John Main when her next two books were published.

There is some disagreement among Elsie's biographers as to how much she helped or hindered Herbert's political career by her radical opinions and unconventional behavior. Much has been written about Elsie and her lovers by these biographers and others, but there is less agreement as to whether Herbert also had an extra-marital affair with the wife of a Washington diplomat. In any case, the rumors must have reached and distressed his father and other members of his more conventional family.

Although Herbert lost in his bid for a fourth term in the elections of 1910, it appears to have had little to do with Elsie's writing or their marital lifestyle. He was one of twelve Republican congressmen in New York who were swept out of office, due in large part to the growing factional conflict between progressives and conservatives in the GOP. Although he also resigned as chairman of the New York Republican County Committee, he remained active in the party for many years.

Herbert returned to his father's law firm, and joined him on the boards of several nonprofit institutions, including the Memorial Hospital, where he became president after his father's death in 1915. Despite their many differences over matters of religion, pacifism and even modesty (Elsie loved to swim in the nude) Herbert and Elsie remained married for twenty-five years. He died in 1925 at the Lenox family farm, Stonover, while demonstrating a new motorcycle he had just bought for one of his sons.

However, life was kinder to the three other Parsons children—Mary and Gertrude, who never married, as well Constance, who was happily married to a lawyer, Montgomery Hare, for many years. Even though so many of the deaths of close family members suffered by Parsons occurred while he was living at either Lounsberry in Rye or Stonover in Lenox, his two country homes remained his beloved retreats.

Chapter Seventeen
Indicted

I n 1909, Parsons faced the greatest legal challenge of his career. At the age of eighty, he was indicted, along with other directors of the Sugar Trust, for actions that the federal government alleged were in restraint of trade and illegal under the Sherman Act. Progressive Era politics were an important factor in the decision by the Taft Administration to pursue this highly publicized case.

In March of that year, William Howard Taft was sworn in as the twenty-seventh president of the United States, succeeding Theodore Roosevelt. Taft, who was well-versed in the antitrust field from his experience as a federal judge, chose a prominent New York lawyer and antitrust expert, George Wickersham, as his attorney general.

Eager to prove that he was a true progressive, Taft set out to better Roosevelt's antitrust record. Over the next four years, his administration filed almost twice the number of lawsuits under the Sherman Act than had been initiated during Roosevelt's seven years in office. Roosevelt, who has been called the "Great Trust Buster," initially supported his successor's policies. However, when Taft authorized a lawsuit to break up U.S. Steel, Roosevelt criticized him for his inability to distinguish between "good" and "bad" trusts.

Aim higher – at Sugar Trust directors (courtesy of Library of Congress)

On April 30, 1909, a distinguished group of Wickersham's fellow New York lawyers gathered for dinner at Sherry's restaurant in New York to hear him speak about his new role as head of the Justice Department. Wickersham told them that Taft and his administration intended to continue the "established policy of a vigorous and impartial enforcement of the law" against trusts. Among those who attended the dinner, according to the magazine *Bench & Bar*, were John Parsons, De Lancey Nicholl, Henry Taft (a brother of the president) and Henry Wise, all of whom soon became participants in two major antitrust cases.

The first case, which went to trial less than a month after the dinner, was a civil suit brought under the Sherman Act by the receiver of a bankrupt Pennsylvania sugar refining company. It charged the Sugar Trust and its directors, including Parsons, with acting in restraint of trade and sought damages of $30 million (the Sherman Act provided for awards up to three times the actual proven damages). The trial had been underway for only two weeks when a settlement agreement was reached, calling for the Sugar Trust to pay roughly $5 million in damages.

The settlement benefitted the Sugar Trust because the amount was relatively small and it disposed of the civil suit. However, the Justice Department was able to use the facts developed in that case to begin preparing a criminal action against the same defendants. The basic facts revolved around a promoter named Adolph Segal, who was in the process of building a sugar refinery in Philadelphia when he ran short of funds to complete it, due to losses he had suffered on some real estate deals.

Through a broker, Segal obtained a large loan from the Sugar

Trust and pledged enough of his shares as collateral to give the Trust effective control over his company. When Segal continued to borrow from other sources, the Sugar Trust directors ordered that his refinery be kept closed until its loan was fully repaid. It was this action that the government contended constituted restraint of trade.

It is hard to understand why Harry Havemeyer, Parsons and the other directors of the Sugar Trust ever had dealings with Segal, whose business reputation was unsavory. In a letter to his friend and adviser, Joseph Choate, Parsons wrote that "Segal was a striker. He had black-mailed the Sugar Company to buy a Camden refinery. He determined to try it again; organized the Pennsylvania Company . . . and made it generally understood that it was to be war on the [Sugar] Company."

Samuel Untermyer, one of Segal's attorneys, was asked in an interview after the settlement whether his client was going to press for the prosecution of the Sugar Trust or the directors. He told the reporters, "What would be the use? The sugar company has been a consistent law-breaker ever since its birth . . . It has robbed the public and ruined its would-be competitors. But it is no better than many of the others in its criminal methods, and not as bad as some . . . It accidentally happens at the moment to be the scapegoat . . ."

There was, however, growing pressure on Wickersham to act. A typical reaction to the settlement appeared in a *New York Press* edi-torial: "The price paid by the trust for running competitors out of business will be far too cheap if the guilty ones escape by the reim-bursement . . . of the ruined refinery." On June 10, 1909, the *Times* reported that, "President Taft is taking a personal interest in the man-ner in which the Sugar Trust compromised the suit against it by the Pennsylvania Sugar Refining Company and is going to find out what prospects there are of a successful criminal prosecution of the trust."

Some alleged that the Roosevelt administration had been reluctant to prosecute the Sugar Trust because of the President's close personal and political ties to Parsons's son, Congressman Herbert Parsons, who was a New York Republican leader. Others contended that Roosevelt's Attorney General Bonaparte refused to take any action against the trust on the ground that the Supreme Court decision in the *Knight* case was a bar to prosecution.

Before the indictment was completed, several prominent New York lawyers attempted to persuade Wickersham that charges of criminal conspiracy would be barred by the three-year statute of limitations. Senator Elihu Root of New York (a long-time friend and legal colleague of Parsons) even met with President Taft in an unsuccessful effort to persuade him to prevent the indictments.

To avoid the statute of limitations, the government's lawyers decided to charge that there was a "continuous crime," specifying various acts used by the defendants to keep Segal's refinery closed. It would then be up to the defense to show that their acts were perfectly legal business decisions made to keep Segal from mismanaging the refinery operation and to protect the value of their security for the loan.

In a *Cosmopolitan* magazine article written at the time of the trial, Charles Norcross claimed that "the Sugar Trust stands revealed as the most lawless of all corporations." However, Norcross also reported that Segal had told a banker, "The sugar trust is cornering the market . . . It is buying all refineries that oppose them and dismantling them. I want five hundred thousand dollars. With that sum I will build a refinery, and they must buy me out."

On July 1, 1909, the Grand Jury indicted Parsons and six other directors of the Sugar Trust (Harry Havemeyer had died in 1907). The indictment contained fourteen counts, each carrying a possible fine of up to $5,000 (equal roughly to $116,000 today) or imprisonment up to one year. An article in the *Brooklyn Eagle* noted that a significant position raised by the counsel for the defendants is "that the statute of limitations would invalidate the indictments."

The trial was assigned to Judge Learned Hand, who was then age thirty-seven and had recently been appointed to the bench by President Taft. Judge Hand went on to serve fifteen years on the federal District Court and another thirty-seven years on the U.S. Circuit Court of Appeals for the Second Circuit. He is considered by many to have been among the most important American jurists who was not appointed to the U.S. Supreme Court.

Representing the defendants was an experienced team of lawyers, including John G. Milburn and William D. Guthrie of New York (their legal legacies survive today in the law firms of Carter, Ledyard & Milburn and Cravath, Swaine & Moore). As the defendants were all represented by counsel, they were excused from appearing at the opening session (Parsons was sick at his home in Lenox). Judge Hand ordered them to appear immediately after the Fourth of July holiday but did not require them to provide any security.

At the outset of the trial, counsel for two of the defendants, who were corporate agents but not directors, filed a motion arguing that the charges against them should be dropped on the grounds that the statute of limitations precluded their prosecution. Their motions were granted by Justice Holt in the Circuit Court, who said: "The government has waited for five years before bringing this prosecution

. . . and, in my opinion, the statute of limitations is a bar to this indictment."

The government quickly appealed the ruling to the U.S. Supreme Court, creating a significant further delay in the prosecution. A Supreme Court ruling in favor of the statute of limitations argument would have been of benefit to Parsons and the other defendants as well. When asked why they did not join in the appeal, Parsons explained that they did not want to win on a technicality, saying, "It wouldn't show good sporting blood. We'll fight this thing out."

Those brave words were directed primarily at hostile members of the press like Judson C. Welliver. He wrote in *Hampton's Magazine* that,

> Parsons is one of the finest types of the lawyer of Big Business, who are punctilious as to matters of personal honesty and morality. But men of this kind suffer from a curious moral strabismus, which makes them unable to see the moral side of business affairs involving relations to the public . . . To the Parsons legal mind, a law is a puzzle, not a prohibition; how to beat it, not how to obey it is the question . . . When Parsons couldn't find a loophole through the law, Havemeyer calmly went ahead and smashed his way through; and no man in America had a more successful career in breaking the law and making it pay.

Not to be outdone, *Cosmopolitan* magazine published an article in 1910 by Charles P. Norcross, who claimed: "There is no desire to drag a man from his grave to answer for his misdeeds, but the history of the

Sugar Trust cannot be written except as the life of Henry O. Have-meyer. The men facing retribution to-day were his puppets. They are being tried for malefactions he instigated and perpetrated . . . Aside from Mr. Havemeyer there was only one man whose voice weighed in the company, and that was John E. Parsons, general counsel."

In condemning "all the rebating, all the false weighing, all the crooked work that went on at the docks" by Sugar Trust employees, Norcross asserted that "no one knew more about the misdeeds of the trust than Havemeyer and Parsons." Noting that each of the seven directors received $50,000 a year, he asserted that, "These directors were paid this amount simply to act as dummies, as is shown by the order to Mr. Heike [secretary of the trust] not to give financial reports to anyone other than the president [Havemeyer]."

When Charles R. Heike was asked at a congressional hearing whether Harry Havemeyer dominated the board, he answered: "Per-haps it was a mistake to call it a one-man concern. But nevertheless, he was the dominating figure." Then in answer to a question whether there were not "other very strong men on the board," such as John E. Parsons, Heike said: "Yes, but he was eminent counsel. He would not be consulted in regard to making sugar, or anything like that."

At another point in the hearing, Parsons testified that Havemeyer had never exerted undue influence on him and the other directors. When a committee member stated that "Mr. Havemeyer . . . dom-inated the trust with his personality," Parsons responded: "I cannot accept the statement that Mr. Havemeyer dominated the company or the board. He never dominated me, and I do not believe he domi-nated any of the important men who were there."

After spending nearly sixty years as a lawyer, Parsons decided to retire at the age of eighty from the practice of law and as general counsel of the Sugar Trust, effective January 1, 1910, followed by his resignation from the board of directors the following June. While waiting for the next stage of the criminal trial to take place, Parsons and his wife managed to spend two months in Europe that summer.

The Supreme Court did not hear the appeal until November 10, 1910, more than a year after the lower court decision. Heading the team of lawyers on the appeal was Joseph H. Choate who argued that a conspiracy is a completed crime as soon as it is formed, even if it leads to acts that occur at a later time.

Counsel for the government argued that it was sufficient to establish the existence of a conspiracy and then prove the overt acts running through the period the conspiracy remained in effect. In an opinion written by Justice Oliver Wendell Holmes, the Supreme Court ruled that the indictment was sound in charging that there was a continuing conspiracy, which was not barred by the statute of limitations. Even though the Supreme Court decision cleared the way for the criminal prosecution to proceed, the trial remained in limbo for many more months.

During the long hiatus in the trial proceedings Parsons continued to deal with Sugar Trust problems. In July of 1911, he testified for nearly six hours before a special congressional committee that was conducting further investigations into violations of the Sherman Act by the Sugar Trust. At the start of his testimony, Parsons said that he had retired from the practice of law and gave his current occupation as "farmer." He then proceeded to answer a wide range of questions from the committee members. When asked about his economic views, he described himself as a "States Rights" man who was strongly opposed to interference by the federal government with the ordinary business of the country.

He contended that the combination he had designed for the Sugar Trust was both legal and good business. When asked if the trust arrangement had not suppressed competition among the combined companies, he responded, "Certainly, but why should partners compete with each other? They should help each other." In answering a similar question from another committee member, Parsons replied that "The big fish swallow up the little fish if the little fish are fools enough to let them do it," adding, "but not if the government will let them do what the government ought to let them do—let them combine."

Several times, committee members alluded to the fact that Parsons was still facing prosecution. At one point, the chairman, Thomas Hardwick of Georgia, seemed to be describing Parsons's own predicament. He suggested that under the Sherman Act, if a man goes into a business enterprise, he may not know whether the act is legal or not until he is in court and a jury decides.

Parsons seized the opportunity to note that if a businessman "gets advice from a lawyer, both he and his lawyer may go to jail." To make his point clear for the record, he added, "That raises the question whether a fair way of interpreting a statute is one that requires the Supreme Court of the United States to consider the matter for months with the result that its decision has been criticized, and whether the fair result should be to punish someone criminally."

There was no further word on the resumption of the trial until Friday, October 13, 1911, when it was reported that the government was ready to proceed with the prosecution. Yet the trial still did not resume until March 11, 1912. In his opening statement that day, U.S.

Attorney Wise invoked the Old Testament, charging that the defendants "were guilty of violating the Tenth Commandment: Thou shall not covet thy neighbor's house."

After Judge Hand denied a motion by the defense to direct a verdict of acquittal, Parsons took the stand in his own defense. The *Times,* which covered the trial on a daily basis, described the scene when Parsons was called to testify: "Taking off his topcoat, the aged defendant made his way to the stand, settled himself comfortably, crossed his legs and prepared for the ordeal. He appeared perfectly at ease."

Parsons then explained the reasons that the Sugar Trust was compelled to take control of the Pennsylvania refinery in order to protect its interests. According to columnist Elbert Hubbard, who was covering the trial for *Hearst's Magazine,* the prosecutor asked Parsons at one point, "What was the price of sugar in 1902?" Parsons slowly answered, "Mr. Wise, my housekeeper does all the marketing. I am a lawyer . . . Anything I did, I did in my office as an attorney, and His Honor knows that, officially, lawyers have poor memories."

As he left the stand at the end of his testimony that day, he was reported to have said with a smile, "A little thing like a criminal prosecution can't hurt me." The following day, Parsons returned to the stand and described how his handling of the Segal loan fulfilled his responsibilities to protect the interests of his client. It was late in the day when defense counsel finished his questioning. By then Parsons had been on the stand for more than four hours.

Even though Parsons said he was willing and able to go on testifying, Judge Hand deferred the rest of the cross-examination. The next day, spectators in the courtroom witnessed a duel of wits between U.S. Attorney Wise and Parsons, an experienced trial lawyer, which resembled a contest between a cobra and a mongoose. Parsons's answers to Wise's questions lasted most of the morning, but when he stepped down, counsel for the defense was well enough satisfied with the result that he rested his case.

After a trial of three weeks, the courtroom was filled to overflowing on March 28 when defense counsel Nicholl made his final statement to the jury. There were many women among the spectators, including a large women's club group that was studying government issues. When both sides had finished addressing the jury, Judge Hand gave them careful instructions on the points of law and instructed them that they could not consider evidence of any events that occurred prior to July 1, 1906, three years before the date of the indictments. The defense had, therefore, hoped for a quick verdict of not guilty.

Hours passed, however, with no indication of any sort coming from the jury room. Parsons did not leave the courtroom during the break for luncheon, remaining there with his counsel and son Herbert. With his usual self-control, he chatted quietly with some friends and showed little sign of the stress he was under.

The jurors began their deliberations in the early afternoon, and as the day wore on, it became apparent that no verdict was imminent. All of the defendants remained in the courtroom, but late in the day Judge Hand granted permission for Parsons to wait for the verdict at his home. Around five o'clock the jury asked Judge Hand for further instructions and were told that they could acquit if the jury found that the defendants had done nothing criminal since July 1, 1906. Finally, at 1:30 on Sunday morning the jury reported that they were unable to agree upon a verdict, so Judge Hand was forced to declare a mistrial and then discharged the jury.

It was learned after the trial ended that the jury stood seven for acquittal and five for conviction in their early voting. However, on their last ballot, only one juror voted for conviction. A key factor in the jury's deliberations was Judge Hand's instruction on the effect of the statute of limitations, which required them to find that any of the criminal acts charged occurred within the three-year period immediately preceding the date of the indictment.

Once again, the prosecutor left the defendants in limbo while he and Attorney General Wickersham took nearly nine months to decide whether to retry them. Most likely, Taft, who was running for reelection against both Roosevelt (Bull Moose Party) and Wilson (Democrat), ordered the delay until after the election in November. He dared not further antagonize the conservative wing of the Republican Party, especially the business community.

During the heated campaign, Roosevelt wrote an article for *Outlook* magazine (later reprinted in his autobiography), in which he criticized Taft's aggressive antitrust policies. Instead, he proposed that, "We should not strive for a policy of unregulated competition . . . Nor should we persevere in the hopeless experiment of trying to regulate these industries by means only of lawsuits . . . We should enter upon a course of supervision, control and regulation of these great corporations . . ."

On December 5, 1912, a month after Wilson won the election, District Attorney Wise appeared before the presiding judge in the Federal District Court in New York and asked that the indictment against Parsons and his co-defendants be dropped. "The government," Wise said, "was unable to prove any affirmative acts by any of the defendants within the three years preceding the date of the return of the indictment. In consulting with the jurors, I was informed that the principal reason why the jury was unable to bring in a verdict was the statute of limitations."

After that self-serving statement, Wise added, "The defendant, John E. Parsons is in his eighty-fourth year. All of the other human defendants are men advanced in years. I am convinced that to bring this case on for trial again would be a useless waste of time and money and could not possibly result in a verdict of conviction." The court granted the U.S. Attorney's motion to quash the indictment, ending the criminal trial. However, the government's civil suit to dissolve the Sugar Trust lasted from 1910 until 1921 when it was finally ended by a consent decree.

The stressful prosecution had finally ended, but the media attacks on Parsons and the other defendants did not immediately cease. Among the most vitriolic of the critics was Charles Norcross, who ended his series of *Cosmopolitan* articles with this sweeping condemnation, aimed primarily at Parsons:

> Thomas, Donner, Senff and others were mere puppets of Havemeyer. Parsons was something more. He has the cunning and brain to plan, the merciless ferocity to execute, and the atrophied conscience that never leaves a pang of remorse. For years he has posed as the leader of the bar, creaking with respectability, oozing oleaginous philanthropy, a lesson and pattern for all to follow. In his old age, he stands at the bar, stripped of his honors, pitilessly exposed as a jackal of commerce and law, whose name will be anathema.

Despite such vilification, Parsons retained the esteem and affection of the people he most valued. At his eighty-fourth birthday dinner celebration on October 24, 1913, he was warmly toasted by fifty of his admirers at Delmonico's. At the dinner, Joseph H. Choate, who was toastmaster, referred in his remarks to the ordeal of trial by "indictment and defamation" that Parsons had suffered. After the death of Parsons, Choate revisited the criminal trial of his great friend in a memorial that he wrote for the bar association's yearbook of 1916, saying: "What a frightful ordeal it was for a man of exalted position, of unblemished character, foremost in his profession, in the church, and in the social world to undergo to suit the changing theories of the courts and of the Government."

Prior to publication, Choate showed a draft of the Parsons memorial to former Attorney General George W. Wickersham, who was then president of the City Bar Association. He wrote Choate, asking him to modify the memorial, because, he said, "certain facts have not been brought to your attention or have been overlooked by you." Wickersham did not state those facts in his letter to Choate, but in a letter written on June 25, 1909, authorizing U.S. Attorney Henry Wise to proceed with the indictment, Wickersham said: "I feel great personal regret that men of the prominence of these gentlemen should be indicted, but the facts under the law, as laid down by the circuit court of appeals seem to justify no other course."

After Choate made some modifications, Wickersham again wrote him to say that, "I did greatly regret the necessity of directing that criminal proceedings be taken against Mr. Parsons . . . I do not know of any act in my official life that was more uncongenial to me, but at the time I thought, and subsequent reflection has entirely convinced me, that no person in the position I occupied could have failed to direct that prosecution without being grossly derelict in the performance of his sworn duty."

Chapter Eighteen
A Gilded Age for Lawyers

Parsons witnessed major changes in the legal profession during his sixty years of law practice. In the period before the Civil War (often called the "golden age" of American law), the prominence of lawyers like Daniel Webster and Rufus Choate prompted Alexis de Tocqueville to write: "In America there are no nobles or literary men, and the people are apt to mistrust the wealthy; lawyers consequently form the highest political class and the most cultivated circle of society."

In the aftermath of the Civil War, however, the legal profession in New York and elsewhere suffered from relaxation of rules for bar admission as well as from a lack of organization and leadership.

Beginning in the 1870s, the nation's economic expansion brought increasing financial success for those at the top of the legal profession, especially in New York City. It was not only the nation's business and financial capital but also the home of the large-circulation newspapers and magazines that helped to publicize and further the careers of Parsons and other leaders of the country's first bar association.

For the first thirty years of his career, Parsons practiced law with only one or two partners, assisted by a succession of law clerks.

DURING A TRIAL

Joseph H. Choate in the courtroom (from *Joseph H. Choate: New Englander, New Yorker, Lawyer, Ambassador*. New York: Dodd, Mead and Company, 1917).

He then flourished as a sole practitioner from 1884 until 1890 but returned to a small firm practice for the last twenty-five years of his long career, while also acting as general counsel for the Sugar Trust. Even at the turn of the twentieth century there were few law firms with more than four or five partners.

However, there was a trend toward larger firms, largely in response to the growing need of their corporate clients for ever more specialized skills to handle the increasingly complex business and financial transactions. According to historian Alfred S. Eichner, the American economy experienced "a momentous organizational convulsion" between 1895 and 1907. Not only did the pace of mergers increase during this period, but, in his opinion, "much more important was the fact that the surviving enterprises were of a radically different nature." This business revolution not only marked the birth of the modern corporation, it also marked the birth of the modern corporate lawyer as well as the modern law firm.

In the 1902 edition of the *World Almanac* Parsons was included among the 646 millionaires listed in New York City (along with 22 other lawyers out of a total of 3,506 nationwide). The financial success of those who were then at the top of the legal profession was far greater than for those practicing law earlier in the century when the greatest advocate of the era, Daniel Webster, ventured that "Most good lawyers work hard, live well and die poor."

In 1908, the *Times* published an article profiling leading lawyers who were especially noted for the large fees they earned for their corporate legal work. The *Times* wrote glowingly of "John E. Parsons, New Yorker born and bred, legal advisor to big corporations and estates, and as a lawyer, believed to have the finest practice in the country."

Also featured was William Nelson Cromwell, who was famous for having earned $1,000,000 from a French corporate client when he negotiated a highly favorable sale of its assets in the area where the Panama Canal was built. A founder of Sullivan and Cromwell, he was called the "physician of Wall Street," who was one of the "new breed of lawyer bred by the growth of great corporations and the most skilled reorganizer of wrecked business enterprises in the legal profession." The *Times* article described Cromwell as a "small, secretive and rather nervous man, who has been compared to a mole for the way he burrows into intricate business problems. He combines a fine legal judgment with brilliant financial skill."

Few, if any, lawyers of the period had as many major corporate clients as John W. Sterling, a founder of Shearman & Sterling. At the time of his death in 1918, he was a director of more than twenty corporations, including numerous banks, railroads and utilities. A life-long bachelor, Sterling left an estate of 20 million dollars, of which 15 million was bequeathed to Yale, his alma mater. At the time, it was the largest sum ever donated to an institution of high learning—equivalent to about 200 million in current dollars. Although he was a highly paid lawyer for many years, his extraordinary wealth was derived largely from astute investing.

Another prominent corporate lawyer was Parsons's good friend, Francis Lynde Stetson, who headed Stetson, Jennings & Russell (ancestor of Davis Polk & Wardwell). In his role as J.P. Morgan's principal legal adviser, Stetson counseled the House of Morgan on numerous industrial and railroad organizations and became general counsel of such major companies as United States Steel Corporation and the Southern Railway.

Elihu Root was also singled out, because, according to the *Times*, "lawyers regard him as probably the greatest corporation lawyer in the United States." Root had managed to retain that reputation even though he was then secretary of the War Department in Theodore Roosevelt's cabinet and had not practiced law in many years. Although not a noted appellate advocate, Root belonged among the select group of corporate lawyers because he was a superb legal technician, who, according to the legal historian, James Willard Hurst, "scorned to become salaried counsel of any economic empire."

A key to Parsons's great success was his ability to find innovative approaches to achieve his clients' goals. He was also skillful in selecting other leading lawyers to help him win cases and settle controversies for his clients. When New York's highest court ordered the dissolution of the Sugar Trust in 1890, Parsons worked out a solution with the noted corporate law experts, John Dos Passos and Elihu Root. Together they crafted a creative reorganization of the Sugar Trust as a holding company under the favorable New Jersey Corporations law. After Ohio outlawed the Standard Oil trust, it and many other corporate trusts quickly joined the holding company parade.

When the federal government filed civil and criminal actions against the Sugar Trust, alleging violation of the antitrust laws, Parsons chose a renowned Philadelphia lawyer, John G. Johnson, as his co-counsel. Together they successfully defended the Sugar Trust all the way to the United States Supreme Court where they won the landmark *Knight* case.

The son of a village blacksmith who had only a high school education, Johnson had the unique distinction of twice declining a seat on the U.S. Supreme Court, first offered by President Garfield and later by President Cleveland. Like Parsons, he believed that his primary duty was to his clients, and that he could best serve his profession and the public by remaining in private practice.

In a commencement address at Harvard in 1905, then president Theodore Roosevelt spoke about the growing public criticism of lawyers who represented big corporations. He told the Harvard graduates: "We all know that . . . many of the most influential and most highly remunerated members of the Bar . . . make it their special task to work out bold and ingenious schemes by which their very wealthy clients, individual or corporate, can evade the laws . . . Now the lawyer who employs his great talent and learning in enabling a very wealthy client to circumvent or override the law encourages the growth within this country of a spirit of dumb anger against all laws and of disbelief in their efficacy."

The growing criticism of the legal profession by opinion leaders like Roosevelt motivated the American Bar Association to develop its first Canons of Professional Ethics, which were adopted in 1908. One of the newly adopted canons was particularly applicable to Parsons when he was indicted in 1909 for his actions as general counsel and director of the Sugar Trust in 1909. Canon 15 stated:

> The lawyer owes entire devotion to the interest of the client, warm zeal in the maintenance and defense of his rights and the exertion of his utmost learning and ability, to the end that nothing be taken or be withheld from him, save by the rules of law, legally applied. No fear of judicial disfavor or public unpopularity should restrain him from the full

discharge of his duty . . . The office of attorney does not permit, much less does it demand of him for any client, violation of law or any manner of fraud or chicane. He must obey his own conscience and not that of his client.

The origins of this canon can be traced to a statement made by Lord Henry Brougham in his defense of Queen Caroline, whose husband (King George IV) sought to annul their marriage. Brougham told the House of Lords: "[An] advocate, in discharge of his duty, knows but one person in all the world, and that person is his client. To save that client by all means and expedients, and at all hazards and costs to other persons, and among them, to himself, is his first and only duty; and in performing this duty, he must not regard the alarm, the torments, the destruction he might bring upon others."

Criticizing Brougham's "doctrine" in his 1907 book, *The American Lawyer*, John Dos Passos wrote: "There perhaps never was language written, or spoken, which contained worse doctrine than that . . . of Brougham, and yet it has been relied on over and over by lawyers to cover all kinds of dishonest practices and defenses . . ." Like Brougham, however, Parsons believed that he owed his highest duty to his clients, and he tolerated the negative press during his criminal trial as the hazard and cost of being a zealous adviser and advocate for the Sugar Trust.

The crux of the criminal trial was a decision by the Sugar Trust board to keep a new refinery from opening until its owner (Segal) repaid a loan in full. Parsons should have followed the advice of his friend Root, who said: "A lawyer's chief business is to keep his clients out of litigation." Or, as Root phrased it on another occasion: "About half the practice of a decent lawyer consists in telling clients that they are damned fools and should stop." However, Harry Havemeyer and the rest of the board did not want to reward the unscrupulous Segal, and Parsons was confident they had the law on their side.

As the trial dragged on, Parsons wrote with frustration to Joseph Choate:

> At this juncture I ask you as a friend and as advisory counsel to consider what, if anything, I personally am called upon to do. Up to now I have been silent (somewhat unwillingly) and acquiescent. I am not concerned about my view of the law. Two Attorneys-General and almost all lawyers have been of the same opinion. What I am concerned about is that there shall not be put upon me responsibility which belongs elsewhere.
>
> As a lawyer, I acted according to my opinion of the law, and for my part must take the consequences. I hold no brief for Mr. Havemeyer. In this transaction, he had the approval of his Board. His act was intended to be, was believed to be, in the interest of the company . . . No officer or director, so far as I know, had any personal interest. I did not benefit even to the extent of fees for legal services . . .

By acting as both as a director and as general counsel of the Sugar Trust, Parsons had significantly increased his risk of civil and criminal liability. However, this dual role had become widely accepted by corporate lawyers by the turn of the century. John Dos Passos noted in his 1907 book: "The lawyer now boldly enters into the business end of his client's transactions—he sells prudence and experience, sometimes usurping the client's discretion and judgment."

One hundred years later, the law firm of Vinson & Elkins was implicated in the criminal activities of Enron, its major client. The firm's defense was that lawyers may assist in a transaction that is not illegal and that has been approved by company management. In so doing, they contended, the lawyers are not approving the business decisions made by the clients. Even though he was general counsel and a director, Parsons might well have asserted the same defense as Vinson & Elkins, because in his mind he was always acting as a lawyer, advising his client how to accomplish what he considered to be legal under the *Knight* decision.

Chapter Nineteen

Summing Up

Despite their very different personalities, John Parsons and Joseph Choate remained close colleagues and friendly rivals for more than sixty years. At Parsons's eighty-fourth birthday dinner celebration in 1913, Choate, the toastmaster, spoke perceptively about their differences: "We took very different views of life and of the business of lawsuits. I thought the great object of a lawsuit was to get all the fun out of it I could, and I generally succeeded; and Mr. Parsons thought that the object was to perform a stern and serious duty to his conscience and his client . . ."

Choate then confessed: "I was always a little afraid of him because of his earnest preparation of his cases, his absolute devotion to his clients. I have heard that on one occasion he said that he was afraid of me because he did not know what I might say next . . . I was always the aggressor; I admit that. And I was very irritating—I think he will acknowledge that; but he was always the conscientious . . . lawyer, seeing to it that the rights of his client were maintained at all hazards, at whatever sacrifice to himself."

Recalling the impeachment of three judges during the "horrible days" of the Tweed era, Choate said that "It was by Mr. Parsons's

Parsons in his seventies (courtesy of Memorial Sloan Kettering Cancer Center)

services . . . that he placed the whole community, the whole country, the whole world under a great debt of gratitude . . . That required courage of the highest order . . . because the people whom he was arraigning were in actual possession of the city government and of its treasury . . ."

He ended his remarks with a reference to the criminal proceedings against Parsons, saying, "I do not believe there is any lawyer at this table who at that time, under the case presented to him, under the law as it then stood, would have given any other advice or opinion than that which he gave on that occasion. And this faithful discharge of duty subjected him to long years of suffering, of which, fortunately, he has survived unharmed . . ."

After that warm tribute, it was surprising that, following Parsons's death, Choate chose to ignore the dictum, *de mortuis nil nisi bonum* ("do not speak ill of the dead") when he wrote a memorial for the 1916 yearbook of the New York City Bar Association. After describing Parsons's "great qualities which essentially fitted him for leadership as an advocate," Choate added, "To these great and valuable qualities, there were two drawbacks, which modified not the success, but, it seems to me, the interest of his long career. He was somewhat lacking in imagination and absolutely without a sense of humor . . ."

Adding insult to injury, Choate continued: "There was a certain rigid formality in his manner and bearing, a coldness of composition, which kept people at a distance, and a very strenuous insistence upon all the rights of his clients, alike in court and in negotiations, which gave the younger members of the profession, who came in contact with him, a feeling that he was much severe and unyielding, and made him, as I think, for a long time generally unpopular with them."

Those disparaging comments, which were quoted in *Causes and Conflicts: The Centennial History of the Association of the Bar of the City of New York* by George Martin, have unfairly left a lasting negative impression of Parsons. Not quoted by Martin is the final paragraph from Choate's memorial: "It would be hard to find in the whole ranks of our profession a more upright and honorable example of true service than the whole history of his life affords, and his name deserves to be cherished forever in this Association, as one of the most zealous founders and most valuable members and servants."

At Parsons's birthday dinner, Elihu Root gave a toast in his honor as a representative of the "junior bar" (he was then sixty-nine but sixteen years younger than Parsons). Everyone in attendance knew of Root's many distinguished achievements as secretary of war and of state as well as a U.S. senator and the recipient of the 1912 Nobel Peace Prize. On this occasion, however, Choate introduced Root simply as "one of Mr. Parsons's own boys, who grew up in his office . . ."

After praising Parsons's talents as a lawyer, Root spoke movingly of his role as a mentor:

> I have always been proud to say and to feel that I had the beginning of my professional career under the tutelage of Mr. Parsons, and if I could use the terms that are familiar in the profession that I have seen a great deal of in recent years, the profession of diplomacy, I should speak of him and to him as I always think of him, as "*mon cher maitre.*"
>
> And more than that, I owe to his intellectual qualities a debt of gratitude for the kindness, consideration and friendship, which it has always been my privilege to enjoy. No one

could be more considerate to a boy just beginning in his profession than he was to all the young fellows in that office . . . I am proud to have been his pupil. I am happy to have the opportunity to tell him in what grateful remembrance, with respect, with honor and with affection I have held him during all the nearly half century since I was a boy in his office . . .

Parsons enjoyed the role of teacher and spent many years as a lecturer at NYU's Law School. Speaking at the University of Pennsylvania Law School in 1901, he said: "The fable of the tortoise and the hare is often illustrated among lawyers. Mere brilliance will never make a lawyer successful in his practice nor useful to his client. Absolute integrity; fidelity to those who entrust him with their interests, a conscientious bestowal of his best efforts to the work at hand—these are the characteristics that will give a lawyer a creditable career, even if he fails to rise to the highest rung of the ladder."

To those outside the circle of his family, friends and colleagues, Parsons's natural reserve could make him appear imposing. A journalist, Dexter Marshall, gave this description of Parsons in 1898 when he was approaching age seventy: "He is tall, spare, but well built, carries his head at a beautiful poise, has clean complexion, trim little sideboards, extremely suggestive of an Englishman's, a straight nose with wide sensitive nostrils, and the coldest, most icy eye that ever looked through a legal proposition, discerning at once its strong points and its weaknesses. Everything about him, even to his mouth and his heavily chiseled jaw, bespeaks strength . . ."

Contrasted with that rather severe description of Parsons was Choate's assertion that "no matter what happened, he was as serene as a summer morning . . . nothing ever could disturb his spirit, and I always thought that was the secret of his success." A *Times* reporter did, however, capture a rare display of public emotion by Parsons during his criminal trial: "The most dramatic moment of the day came as Mr. Nicholl [Parsons's attorney], in his peroration, referred to the long and honored career of John E. Parsons, the principal defendant, and asked the jury how they could send his gray hairs in dishonor to the grave. As he spoke, the marvelous self-control of Mr. Parsons at last broke down, and he wept, and his son, Herbert Parsons, wept with him."

When he was relaxed, however, Parsons could be quite charming and witty. Elbert Hubbard, a columnist for *Hearst's International*, talked with Parsons just after a grueling day of testifying at his criminal trial, and reported that, "Parsons was courteous, gracious and the youngest man of his years [age 83] I had ever seen." When asked, "What is the secret to your perpetual youth?" Parsons replied, with his dry sense of humor: "I do not overeat, and I do not overhate. I keep busy, am interested in every human endeavor and enjoy life."

Stories about Parsons's self-discipline were legendary among reporters, including one who wrote: "In spite of his great earnings and in spite of his metropolitan appearance, John E. Parsons is not generally supposed to be fond of the good things in life. In fact, he is believed to be what a New Englander would call 'near.' This belief . . . is based chiefly on the fact that he is known at least once to have made his lunch in the courtroom during a case . . . composed of a single buttered roll brought to court in his coattail pocket, wrapped in a fringed doily."

The only non-lawyer who spoke at Parsons's birthday celebration in 1913 was the rector of the Episcopal Church in Lenox, William Grosvenor. He told the more than fifty lawyers and other guests,

> I think of Mr. Parsons with an old hat on, walking along the beautiful roads and lanes of Lenox and the Berkshires, with a tall staff in his hand, caring, really caring for every person and everything in the community, interested in the uplift of every part of the life of that village.
>
> And that deep personal interest took the outward form of several institutions. A beautiful chapel, a Parish House, and the very useful summer home, where hundreds of children have enjoyed their vacation days. His charities in New York are well known. The Brick Church, the whole Presbyterian Church in the United States, the Woman's and the Memorial Hospitals, Cooper Union and many other institutions have had his loyal and generous support.

Yet, Parsons was not content to rest just on his lifetime achievements. Dr. William Reed Huntington, a long-serving rector of Grace Church in New York City, recalled that Parsons once asked his guests at a dinner party to say what their idea of heaven was, and when it came his turn, Parsons said he thought it was a place where there was lots of work to do.

Asked by Elbert Hubbard in 1912 how long he expected to live, Parsons's answer was: "I am willing to go or stay; I am not preparing to die, I am preparing to live." Less than a year later, the *Times* carried the following article:

The most distinguished walking club in America has just been organized in New York. The charter members are Mayor William Gaynor, Joseph H. Choate, former ambassador to Great Britain; William B. Hornblower, John E. Parsons (the Nestor of the New York Bar) and Lewis Windmuller. A few of those said to be contemplating making an application for membership are Andrew Carnegie, Andrew N. Seligman, Jacob H. Schiff, Surrogate Fowler, Gen. George W. Wingate and Karl Pickardt . . . The club will be known as the Pedestrians Club, whose main object is the furthering of the fine art of walking right here in New York . . . The combined age of the charter members is 367 years . . .

The news of the club's formation was announced at the Mayor's office yesterday, along with the information that some fine day soon no one should be surprised to read of a hike by all the charter members beginning at City Hall Park and ending somewhere in Bronx Park or Coney Island or Ft. Hamilton. They may even hike all the way to Yonkers, it was said.

Bibliography

Amory, Cleveland. *The Last Resorts*. New York: Harper, 1952.

Baird, Charles W. *Chronicle of a Border Town—History of Rye, Westchester County, New York, 1660–1870*. New York: Anson D.F. Randolf and Company, 1871.

Baker, Ray Stannard. *The Spiritual Unrest*. New York: Frederick A. Stokes Company, 1910.

Beard, Charles A. and Mary R. *The Rise of American Civilization*. New York: Macmillan, 1930.

Bird, Isabella Lucy. *The Englishwoman in America*. London: John Murray, 1856.

Burrows, Edwin G. and Mike Wallace, ed. *Gotham: A History of New York City to 1898*. New York: Oxford University Press, 1999.

Cooper, James Fenimore. *The Spy: a Tale of the Neutral Ground*. New York: Charles Wiley, 1824.

Dalphin, Marcia. *Fifty years of Rye:1904–1954*. Rye, NY: City of Rye, 1955.

Dos Passos, John. *The American Lawyer*. New York: The Banks Law Publishing Co., 1907.

Eichner, Alfred S. *The Emergence of an Oligopoly: Sugar Refining as a Case Study*. Baltimore: The Johns Hopkins Press, 1969.

Hammack, David C. *Power and Society: Greater New York at the Turn of the Century*. New York: Russell Sage Foundation, 1982.

Hardy, Iza Duffus. *Between Two Oceans: Or Sketches of American Travel*. London: Hurst and Blackett, 1884.

Harrison, Mrs. Burton. *Recollections Grave and Gay*. New York: Charles Scribner's Sons, 1916.

Havemeyer, Harry W. *Henry Osborne Havemeyer—The Most Independent Mind*. New York: Privately Printed, 2010.

————. *Merchants of Williamsburgh*. New York: Privately Printed.

Holzer, Harold. *Lincoln at Cooper Union: The Speech That Made Lincoln President*. New York: Simon & Schuster, 2006.

Howells, William Dean. *Impressions and Experiences*. New York: Harper & Brothers, 1896.

Jackson, Jr., Richard S. and Cornelia Brooke Gilder. *Houses of the Berkshires: 1870–1930*. New York: Acanthus Press, 2011.

James, Henry. *Washington Square*. New York: Harper & Brothers, 1880.

Kimball, LeRoy, ed. "A Student at New York University in 1847: Excerpts from the Diary of John E. Parsons," The New York Historical Society Quarterly, vol. 38 No. 3 (July, 1954): reprinted by the New York University Alumni Association, 1954.

Koblenz, Lawrence. *From Sin to Science: The Cancer Revolution in the Nineteenth Century*. Unpublished PhD dissertation, 2013.

Lamoreaux, Naomi R. *The Great Merger Movement in American Business: 1895-1904*. Cambridge: Cambridge University Press, 1985.

Martin, George. *Causes and Conflicts: The Centennial History of the Association of the Bar of the City of New York, 1870–1970*. New York: Fordham University Press, 1997.

McCabe, James D. *Lights and Shadows of New York Life*. Philadelphia: The National Publishing Co., 1872.

Mullins, Jack Simpson. *The Sugar Trust: Henry O. Havemeyer and the American Sugar Refining Company*. Unpublished PhD dissertation, 1954.

Panetta, Roger G. *Westchester: The American Suburb*. New York: Fordham University Press, 2006.

Parsons, Elsie Clews. *The Family: An Ethnographical and Historical Outline with Descriptive Notes*. New York: G.P. Putnam's Sons, 1906.

Parsons, John E., Family Papers. New York Historical Society. http://www.nyhistory.org/.

Parsons, John E., Family Papers. Rye Historical Society, Rye, New York.

Roosevelt, Theodore. *An Autobiography.* New York: Macmillan, 1913.

Smith, Matthew Hale. *Sunshine and Shadow in New York.* Hartford: J.B. Burr and Company, 1868.

Strong, George Templeton. *The Diary of George Templeton Strong*, ed. Allan Nevins and Milton H. Thomas. New York: Macmillan, 1952.

Tarbell, Ida M. *The Tariff in our Times.* New York: Macmillan, 1911.

Twiss, Benjamin R. *Lawyers and the Constitution: How Laissez-Faire Came to the Supreme Court.* Princeton, NJ: Princeton University Press, 1942.

Van Wyck, Frederick. *Recollections of an Old New Yorker.* New York: Liveright, Inc., 1932.

Wharton, Edith. *A Backward Glance.* New York: D. Appleton Century, Inc., 1934.

————. *The Age of Innocence.* New York: D. Appleton Company, 1920.

————. *The House of Mirth.* New York: Charles Scribner's Sons, 1904.

Wingate, George W. *History of the Twenty-second Regiment of the National Guard of the State of New York.* New York: E.W. Dayton, 1896.

Index

Page references in *italics* refer to photos and illustrations.